HOW TO DEVELOP YOUR PSYCHIC POWERS

HOW TO DEVELOP YOUR PSYCHIC POWERS

An Introductory Guide

TARA WARD

ARCTURUS

Published by Arcturus Publishing Limited
For Bookmart Limited
Registered Number 2372865
Trading as Bookmart Limited
Desford Road
Enderby
Leicester
LE9 5AD

This edition published 1997

Printed and bound in Great Britain

ISBN 1 900032 66 X

CONTENTS

INTRODUCTION

How many times in your life have you said of yourself 'I must be psychic?' When you were thinking of someone and a moment later they rang you or you bumped into them in the street? When you knew someone was going to say or do something just before they did it? Or was it when you had that feeling of 'déjà vu': when something happens that you know has already happened in a dream? The examples are endless and, no, they aren't just coincidences. The truth is we all have psychic powers. It isn't some 'special' or 'supernatural' gift possessed by only a chosen few. Nor should it be confused with witchcraft or magic spells or sorcery. It is a gift with which we are born and we have the choice either to develop it or to let it lie dormant. The reason this isn't openly obvious to us lies in the fact that this is a gift to be used with respect. You need to develop certain skills before you can practise psychic work safely. However, treated sensitively and responsibly, psychic work isn't just enjoyable, it can also be wonderfully rewarding.

This book is intended for those of you who are just starting on the psychic path. Perhaps you have already read something on the subject or heard something or discussed psychic phenomena with friends, or perhaps you just have a general, nagging feeling that there is more out there in the world than meets the eye. Perhaps you feel as though part of you isn't being used, or maybe you're just curious. Hopefully, this book will at the very least set you thinking about aspects of life which you hadn't considered before and, at very most, set some of you on the path of psychic awareness which may become a fundamental part of your lives.

Start off by asking yourself how you would define the word 'psychic'. If you can, ask other people what they think. Of course, you'll get differing answers but chances are the word 'supernatural' will appear in many of them. Even dictionaries have varying definitions from 'someone claiming to have unusual mental powers', 'concerning the mind rather than the body', 'having to do with soul and mind', 'having knowledge and mental abilities impossible to explain using present scientific understanding' to that popular word that crops up time and again: 'paranormal'. And what does paranormal mean? 'Outside man's normal experience'. Just think: a century ago, the television, telephone and radio, to say nothing of computers, would all have come under the heading of 'paranormal'!

Much of what is discussed in this book is considered common knowledge in Eastern philosophies. Indeed, they have been practising what we call 'psychic behaviour' as a routine matter for centuries. Perhaps it's finally time for Western civilisation to catch up, although it's proving a gradual process for us. Fortunately most of us are now used to hearing the words 'New Age' and 'spiritual awareness' and subjects at which we would have scoffed even a few years ago are gradually becoming more and more accepted. Some concepts in this book may take a bit of time to digest and some you may frankly find indigestible but you're advised simply to try to read with an open mind. What initially seems confusing or implausible will soften with re-reading into a possibility or a clarification of thought. Did you know it's scientific fact that we as human beings only use a very small proportion of our brain: some say as little as fifteen percent? It may help you to bear that thought in mind as you read. Perhaps this book is an opportunity to use just that tiny bit more!

Some of you will be tempted in reading this book to rush through the early passages which relate to the chakras and exercises, anxious to get on to the 'good bit' of actually trying out your psychic powers. However, doing so will only hamper your progress. Psychic work is a very powerful phenomenon and unless you understand some ground rules before you start, it could prove a very confusing and even distressing experience. You can liken it to learning how to drive: that very first moment when you get behind the wheel of a car and all you really want to do is take off and zoom down the road. It's frustrating not to be able to do that but you know if you try it, you're likely to end up in a nasty accident. Well, plenty of 'psychic accidents' can occur, too, if you don't take 'lessons'. Also, if you only half-do the exercises and jump forward in the book, your psychic strength will be diminished and you'll be disappointed with your results. In fact, if you want to get the maximum effect from this book, the best thing you can do is to thoroughly read through the entire book first, without trying any of the exercises. Then re-read it and start the exercises second time around. Or try the exercises on the first reading, but then notice how much more effective you are when you re-do them, having read through the whole book. There isn't any easy short-cut to psychic development but, treated properly, the whole learning process can be a thoroughly enjoyable and exciting one. This book is intended as a fun and safe beginner's guide so that your first psychic experiences, instead of being uncomfortable or distressing, prove to be wonderfully rewarding, encouraging and enlightening, opening up your mind to a whole new realm of possibilities.

Chapter 1
WHAT USE CAN MY PSYCHIC ABILITIES BE?

It's important to look at what you really want to get out of developing your psychic abilities because the clearer you are, the more it will help your progress. Everyone reading this will be at different stages in their psychic growth and by aiming towards your own goals, it will help focus yourself.

Let's start by looking at what psychic development can do for everybody. Do any of the following appeal to you?

1 It's a great form of discipline so it can strengthen and focus your mind.
2 It's a 'mind-expanding' experience to help increase your awareness of the universe.
3 It can be a means of replenishing your own energy, to leave you refreshed and better balanced.
4 It can teach you how to protect yourself better on a day-to-day basis and not be 'drained' by influences around you.
5 It will enable you to 'tune in' to other people so you can develop a greater understanding of them.
6 By enabling you to 'read' other people, it means you can learn more about yourself and those around you.
7 It can be a form of healing to comfort others.
8 It can be used as guidance to help sort out problems.
9 It can be an unselfish, loving act of giving to others and helping others.
10 It's an affirmation of life 'on the other side' which eases the stress of bereavement.

If any of the above inspire you, then you're on the right track. Decide which of the above really matter most to you and on which you'd like to concentrate.

Now have a look at a few things psychic development can't do for you:

1 Predict the future with certainty (it can only give probability patterns because everyone has power over their own life to change things)
2 Provide a fast answer to all life's problems
3 Create a good laugh while you fool around with different people and different psychic phenomena
4 Give you power over other people to make them do what you want them to do.

This last point is particularly important because it's very tempting, once you start discovering your strength, to want to use psychic means to change people around you! Whether it's for your own personal gain or theirs, it won't work.

To look at why this is so, you need to understand 'karma': cause and effect. The expression 'as you sow, so shall you reap' is part of the same belief: that is, that every deed we do, good or bad, will rebound back at us, good or bad. If you haven't thought of this concept before, take a little time to consider it. How often have you done something good for someone and they, or someone else, have returned the compliment without asking? Or have you woken up in a bad mood one day, felt antagonistic towards everyone, and had everyone be aggressive in exchange? What we give out to others is what we receive back ourselves. So any action or thought you take to psychically manipulate someone else, will only rebound back at you, usually in an unpleasant way. It isn't always an immediate pay-off either but you can guarantee it will happen.

Here are a few examples. Have you found any of these happening to you? You were in a relationship where you hurt your partner through thoughtless action. In your next relationship, your new partner did to you exactly what you did to your previous partner. In your work environment, you metaphorically trampled over someone to further your career. A while later, another person trampled over you in a similar fashion. As a teenager, you were rebellious and unkind to your parents. Did you then have a child who behaved that way during their adolescence? Once you start thinking, you'll no doubt have many 'cause and effect' examples in your own life. Karma also rebounds in a wonderfully positive way, of course, although sometimes you may feel your good actions aren't always reciprocated. The reason for this makes the whole concept more complicated, bringing in re-incarnation and how your karma travels with you through different lives. This is also important for your psychic development so you need to take a moment to think of this. Do you believe we all have separate spirits or souls that live on after our physical body has died and that we can 're-incarnate' in other bodies through time? If you can't believe this, it won't stop you from developing your psychic abilities but it will make your progress slower and there will come a point where you can't proceed any further. However, we are all at different stages so where you are now is hopefully different from the place you will be in after reading this book.

It's necessary at least to make the distinction between our physical body and our spiritual one. Most of us know our physical body quite well: its shape, strengths, limitations and uses. But we're only just learning about our spiritual abilities and because they're not so visible or material, it's more difficult for us to grasp. We've also all programmed our brain to distrust what we cannot see and that is a deep-rooted conditioning which we are just starting to change.

It's no coincidence that you're reading this book now. It's because the time is right for you to expand your awareness and stretch yourself in new directions. Of course, you may not understand or agree with everything you read but you will still have increased your knowledge on some level.

One last word on the subject of psychic uses. As you work with your new abilities, you will appreciate how much of the initial work is about tuning in to others and their emotional, mental and physical states. This is a signficant part of our development because so often what we say of others and their current situation can apply to how we lead our own lives. It's believed that we attract to ourselves what we need to learn and grow. So by giving a 'reading' to someone, you will often learn a great deal about yourself. That doesn't mean you should think of yourself as you are actually doing the reading because that is a selfish act and doesn't belong in psychic work. But after you've finished, have a little quiet time to yourself to contemplate what you have offered to that other person. How much of it relates to you? How could you make that advice benefit your own life? It's so true that it's much easier to give advice than to be the one who acts upon it. Psychic development work gives you a good opportunity to stop and think on that level.

Chapter 2
HOW PSYCHIC ENERGIES WORK

At this stage you need to consider whether you want to start your development by working with someone else or on your own. Both have advantages. Two or more people can encourage each other and increase confidence levels. Also it means one person could volunteer to read and guide the other through the exercises, which in the beginning saves you from memorising them on your own. Obviously it's less lonely to share the new experience with someone else. Conversely, if the match isn't right, you can inhibit each other. As we all work at different rates and in different ways, that can lead to confusion initially and make one of you feel less talented than the other. Sometimes in the early stages you can feel rather silly sitting there, waiting for something to happen, and unless you feel safe and comfortable with the other person, you may stop your own progress. Are you more secure on your own or do you prefer to share with others? Are you frightened of feeling an idiot in front of others or do you think there's safety in numbers? Think about how you work best and what feels right for you. If you decide you would like to work with another person, choose them carefully. Do you feel comfortable alone in a room with them? Are they really interested in psychic development? Can you both find some uninterrupted time together? If you've made the decision to work with someone, ensure that you both read the book. It isn't a good idea for just one of you to read it and pass on the information because you may unwittingly leave out vital detail.

Once you've sorted that out, the next stage is to learn some basic details. Just as when you start driving a car, you need to know the fundamental parts of the car: ignition,

The Seven Major Chakras

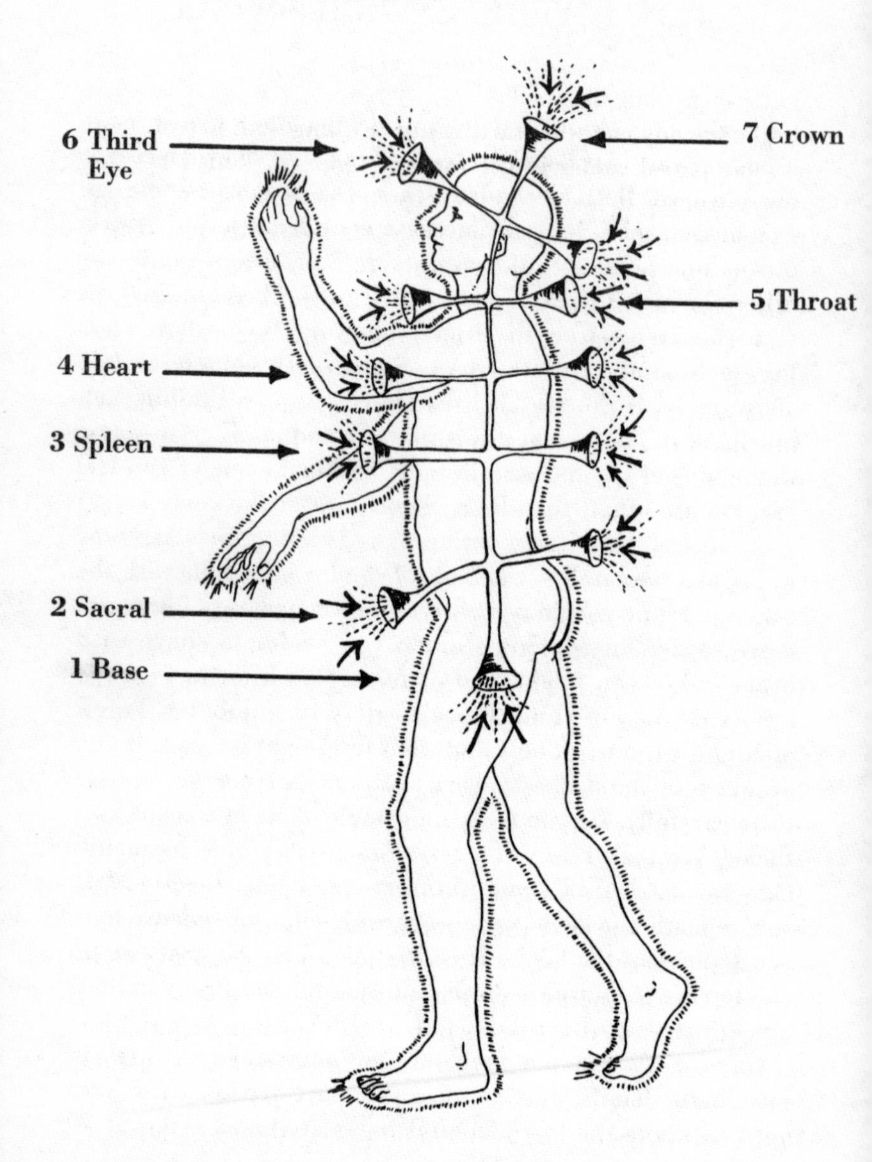

gears, indicators etc., so you need to know about the fundamental parts of psychic work. Although our spiritual make-up is infinitely more complicated than a car engine, it's enough at this stage for you to learn a few basics about how our 'psychic engine' works.

Before any car will start, it needs filling with petrol. Our psychic petrol comes in the form of 'energy'. This isn't the sort of energy it takes to jump up and make a cup of tea or to do a mental task at work. This is a far finer, subtler energy that exists all around us and is perpetually there for us to draw upon. Unfortunately so few of us do this, which is such a waste and part of the reason why many of us go through each day feeling tired and uninspired. Forget the adrenalin rush of caffeine or chocolate; once you've tuned into the universal energy and discovered how to channel it properly, it's far more rewarding!

There's a difference between this universal energy and the energy that exists around humans and objects. (The latter we call the 'aura' but we'll discuss that in detail in the next chapter). The energy we call upon to help us activate our psychic abilities is pure, infinite in supply and comes from a higher source in the universe. Much has been written about this cosmic energy but for our purposes it's sufficient to know that it is always there for us and often symbolised by a pure white light streaming down from above. You may have seen this depicted in paintings, usually in a religious context. We call upon this energy by firstly visualising it, thereby becoming conscious of it and then drawing it into our system to use. Don't worry if this already seems impossible to you: upcoming exercises will show you it's not as daunting as it sounds! So this energy source is our psychic petrol.

Next, you need a key to put in the ignition to fire the engine, and likewise we have to 'ignite' ourselves with outside energy before we can work with our psychic powers. Our key in the ignition comes in the form of our mind opening up our 'chakras', also known as our energy centres, but unlike a car which has only one ignition we have seven major ones! (There has been recent speculation about a possible eighth major chakra, located between heart and throat, but longstanding, traditional methods still favour the seven major ones. There's also a host of minor chakras but you don't have to study those for this level of work). The seven major chakras are of equal importance and all need to be 'fired' to produce a beneficial flow of energy for psychic work. A highly developed psychic can open all seven throttles within a second but a beginner takes considerably longer.

These seven chakras are your gateway into a new world and you need to learn, at the very least, their name, location, colour, and how they 'open'. These seven energy centres are a fascinating subject and worthy of a book on their own. Many years ago, their existence was not even discussed but only handed down from spiritual teacher to student in a highly revered tradition. It really is worth studying the chakras in some depth but there is only space here for a brief, simplified summary.

These seven chakras are all interconnecting centres which flow through the body. Look at the chakra diagram to see how this works. The chakras are cone-like in shape with streams of energy whirling in through the open part of the cone and flowing through the body via connecting 'pipes'. As you study the diagram, imagine pure, white light and energy whirling like a vortex into the cones and then filling your body with light and energy. This is what you will be doing through exercises. Notice how the first chakra (at the base of the spine) and the seventh chakra (at the crown) open upward and downward and connect through to each other. The other five in the middle open both front and back through the body, the second through your solar plexus, the third through your spleen, the fourth through your heart, the fifth through your throat and the sixth through your forehead. You have to learn how to open these energy centres and draw in the energy to be able to practise psychic work. If this last paragraph and the diagram still mean nothing to you, please study both in detail again before continuing. Don't move on until you feel comfortable with the concept. Now let's look at the chakras in more detail.

The word chakra comes from the Indian Sanskrit, meaning 'wheel'. It's helpful to know because each cone spins like a wheel as we open the energy centre. The chakra is also likened to the lotus, which is a beautiful flower, similar to a lily, with many petals. Opening the chakra is also like opening the petals of a flower, an analogy we use during the upcoming exercises. Each chakra has its own colour and is linked to part of our anatomy. Each has its own action associated with it and emotion. That is as deep as we will go for the purposes of this book but their meaning is also much more complex, with animal and elemental symbols allocated to them, different numbers of petals corresponding to different vortices, as well as individual mantras and yantras (mystical dialogues between divinities), used for meditative enlightenment. However, back to our basics. Let's now look at each chakra individually. It's possible that even the raw basics of what is written below will confuse many because it's a new concept for a lot of people. Don't worry if it doesn't make sense initially. Just keep reading and re-reading. There's a re-cap at the end of this chapter to give you the salient points which you need to remember before proceeding.

The First is the Base chakra. Its colour is Red. It's located at the Base of the Spine. This opens downwards to the ground, not front and back. This energy centre is in fact always 'open' but when we do psychic work it needs to be opened more. It's a bit like a fan that's twirling on low speed and needs to be switched onto high. This base chakra is about the physical, earth part of us and relates to our primal instinct of survival. Its physical connection is to the large intestines and excretion, as well as functions of the legs, feet and bones. It's often referred to as the root of ourselves. Because this chakra is all about the physical, the action associated with it is 'I have'. Its state is stillness.

The Second is the Sacral or Solar Plexus chakra. Its colour is Orange. It's located around the Navel. This opens front and back through the body. This centre is not usually open and we have to 'crank it up' as we start. The solar plexus chakra relates to our sexuality and reproductive life and concerns our relationships with others, our ability to share and be intimate. Physically it's connected to the reproductive system, the urinary tract and the menstrual cycle in females and the testes/prostatic plexus in males. This chakra is also called the 'feeling centre', taking in our emotions, and therefore it's associated with 'I feel, I want'. Its state is desire and tears.

The Third is the Spleen chakra. Its colour is Yellow. Its location is the most difficult to explain clearly but it's approximately five inches above the navel and slightly to the left. Because of its location, some teachers invert the second and third chakras and if you read other books on the subject, they may call the spleen the second chakra and the solar plexus the third. For our purposes, we'll stick to our method and if it helps you to imagine the spleen directly above the navel to keep all the energy centres in a straight line, please do so. Through the early learning stages, it won't matter a great deal. This chakra opens front and back but is not naturally open all the time. The spleen energy centre represents our sense of self, our purpose, destiny and willpower. Physically it relates to our digestive system, liver, spleen and stomach. This centre is also very much about our emotions but as they relate to self-will and determination, so it's hardly surprising we use the action 'I can' for this one. Its related states are anger, joy and laughter.

The Fourth is the Heart chakra. Its colour is Green. It's located in the Middle of the Breastbone, Above the Chest, and opens front and back. While the first three chakras we've discussed are about our basic needs and emotions, this now is where our energy vibration starts to change, become a little finer. To explain it using a material example, you could say the first three chakras are like heavy cotton, medium weight and light cotton, and now we are getting on to a finer silk stage. This is not to say one chakra is any better or of more use than another; all have to work together to achieve a harmonious balance. Again, this chakra is not normally open and we have to open it for psychic work. This centre is about compassion and understanding and acts as a sort of hinge between our base levels and our higher, mental levels. We all think of the heart as love but in this context the heart chakra isn't just about love in our relationships, it's also to do with a larger, universal love that is unconditional and limitless. On a physical level, this centre relates to the circulatory system. Its action is 'I love' and its states, naturally enough, are love and compassion.

The Fifth is the Throat chakra. Its colour is Blue. It's located at the Hollow of the Throat and it also opens front and back. This chakra again becomes even finer in vibration than the heart and it's connected to speech, communication, creativity and self-expression. It's not just about our ability to chatter away, however, but about our purifying speech and considering carefully how we speak and the purpose of speech. It's to do with lisening to our own inner voice and meditation. It's also part of sound and vibrations. The throat centre's physical connection is to the respiratory system and its action is 'I speak'. Its state is expansion and excitement.

Expansion is an important part of this chakra: its colour blue can be likened to the limitless expanse of the sky.

The Sixth is the Third Eye chakra. Its colour is Purple or Indigo. Its location is the Middle of the Forehead and it again opens front and back. You may already have heard references to the third eye before or the 'eye of the mind' and this chakra takes us on to yet a greater spiritual realm and higher functions of consciousness. It's connected with intuition and far-seeing knowledge, as well as dreams and memories. This finely-tuned energy centre is not directly related to a physical system within the body the way the other chakras are. Rather it is attuned to the mind, eyes and brain and comes under the heading of 'cognition'. Again, we're not talking about the sort of knowing that comes from a material source but a higher degree of wisdom and vision, attainable only through spiritual development. As meditative processes become all-important here, so the action is 'I see' and the state one of dreaming.

The Seventh is the Crown chakra. Its colour is Violet or White. It's located at the Top or Crown of the Head and it opens upwards. It's through this chakra that we initially draw in the pure white energy which was mentioned earlier in this chapter. This centre, like the base chakra, is always open but again, it whirls on a low frequency and we have to speed it up before we can work effectively with our psychic powers. This is the highest and finest of vibrational energies and is related to self-realisation, fulfilment and enlightenment. It also represents completion as it is the highest state and can only function in the fullest sense with a truly open mind, using truth and sincerity. Because of its heightened state, it is not related to any physical system in the body. Its related action is 'I know' and its state is Bliss. That state known as bliss can only be achieved through prolonged spiritual growth and is outside the comprehension of most of us. For now, it's enough to consider it a concept towards which we can strive!

So those are the seven major chakras, or energy centres, which we need to open in order to draw in the pure, white energy that we can then in turn use for psychic development. As already mentioned, don't worry if you can't remember everything about the chakras at this stage. You can re-cap over the bits you really need to remember at the end of the chapter.

Psychic work can be roughly divided into two categories. The first, the emotional, relates to the first three chakras, the base, solar plexus and spleen, and also, in part, to the fourth, the heart chakra, which has already been described as a 'hinge' between the base and higher levels. This emotional level of psychic work allows us to develop skills such as psychometry, auric reading, flower reading, crystal ball reading, healing, psychic drawing, Tarot cards and the Runes. This is all done on an emotional, feeling wave-length and this is the level we will be studying in this book. The second, higher level is called the mental sphere, which involves use of the finer vibrational frequencies of the throat, third eye and crown chakras, together, again, with the heart centre. Work on this level is purely with 'spirit', via clairvoyance, clairaudience, inspirational speaking and trance work. This we're not going to study in this volume. You need to have a good working knowledge of the emotional levels before venturing into the mental spheres. To make another analogy with driving: it would be the equivalent of just passing your normal driver's test, but then hopping behind the wheel of a double-decker bus or a ten-ton lorry and trying to weave through heavy traffic.

However, because we are not actively using the throat, third eye and crown chakras in our emotional psychic work, it doesn't mean we leave these energy centres closed. All chakras need to be opened to allow the proper flow of energy throughout our body. What we won't be doing is concentrating exclusively on those areas and as you'll discover once we start the exercises, it's easier to start the flow through the base, solar plexus, spleen and heart chakras as the other three chakras require a greater discipline before they can be used fully.

There's one other point you need to consider before we sum up. What is the source of this pure energy we draw into our systems for psychic work? To many people, this has a religious or deeply spiritual foundation, and they would call the pure energy a gift from God, or even God himself. It doesn't matter what you call this source of light: God, Allah, Buddha, Great Universal Spirit – true psychic work is not affiliated to any set religion or belief. Anyone can embrace it. For that reason, when it's suggested in further chapters that you may wish to say a small prayer to acknowledge thanks or to ask for help in psychic development, it's left to you to decide to whom you are speaking. Whoever you believe to be the source of this energy, is the person/entity to whom you should give thanks and appreciation, but no one should tell you who that person is and that you can only pray to one god. Your own deeply personal belief in a good, pure spirit who guides, loves and protects you, is all that is necessary for successful development.

So, to sum up, this is what you really need to know so far: that we draw pure, universal energy into our bodies through our chakras to enable us to work with that energy and develop our psychic abilities. Below is the very least you need to memorise about the chakras (but if you can remember more from earlier in this chapter, it can only benefit you):

1 Base. Red. Base of spine. Opens up and down.
2 Solar Plexus. Orange. Near navel. Opens front and back.
3 Spleen. Yellow. Above and slightly left of navel. Opens front and back.
4 Heart. Green. Centre of breastbone, above chest. Opens front and back.
5 Throat. Blue. Hollow of throat. Opens front and back.
6 Third Eye. Purple. Middle of forehead. Opens front and back.
7 Crown. Violet or White. Top of head. Opens up and down.

You may already have realised the colours are the colours of the rainbow but in case you need it clarified, the green referred to is a grass green and the blue a sky blue.

Chapter 3
DISCOVERING THE AURA AND FURTHER 'ENERGIES'

Before we start our exercises to 'open up' and practise psychic work, there's another subject we need to cover: the aura. The aura is mentioned a lot in this book and you need to develop an understanding of what it is before we go further. Put simply, the aura (sometimes called the human energy field) is a field of energy surrounding our body. It's not normally visible to the layman but it can be seen once we increase our psychic abilities. You've probably all been aware of people's auras at some time or other, even though you may not have actually seen one yet. Has a person ever come and sat next to you on the train or walked into a room and you've felt a change in atmosphere? This is you reacting to someone's aura. Every living object has one (so do inanimate objects, but we'll come to that later) and this aura is constantly changing, expanding and contracting, fluctuating with our emotional, mental, spiritual and physical states.

Have you noticed that when someone is head-over-heels in love, they seem to exude a warmth, a joy, that far exceeds their physical body? Or likewise, when someone loses their temper, you can almost see a red or black glow emanating from them?

If you still aren't sure about this, here's a simple exercise to start you experiencing this unseen energy. Open your palms and fingers flat and place them about twelve inches apart, palm facing palm. Now, slowly, move your hands in towards each other (if you rush this, you're unlikely to feel anything). Try to breathe rhythmically and deeply as you gradually move the palms together. Don't worry if it takes a few attempts before you feel anything because the more relaxed you are, the easier it'll be to get a response. At some point, before your palms touch, you should feel something – a little tingle, a pressure, a warmth, a butterfly tickly feeling, or possibly a stronger sensation of force – it will be different for different people. However it manifests itself to you, this is your own energy fields touching. You can then practise moving your hands slowly back and forth and 'play' with that ball of energy. When does the feeling weaken – or disappear? Does it get stronger the more you experiment with it? You can also practise finger to finger. Then take an index finger and draw circles in the palm of the other hand, without actually touching the skin. Does it tickle?

Our energy field, or aura, is highly intricate and although we can't study it in detail here, you should know that there are at least seven levels or bands to the aura, each radiating out sequentially from the body, and each relating to a different chakra. The first layer relates to the base chakra, the second to the solar plexus and so on. Do you remember the cones we talked about in the previous chapter? In fact, there isn't just one cone front and back; each layer of the aura has its own pair of cones and they all nestle into each other, like a stack of empty icecream cones, through the seven layers. Because of the aura's complexity, some teachers will simplify it into just three basic sections. Only a highly developed psychic is ever likely to see the aura in its entirety and to study this is a lifetime's work. The only level it is likely that a novice will see is the first level, known as the etheric field and this is the band which immediately surrounds us, extending two inches or so from our physical body. Because it's the most dense (in other words, on the least finest vibration) it's possible during the early stages for you to see it as a hazy vapour around the body.

You may still be confused about expressions used in this book such as 'finer vibration' and 'higher frequency' so here's another physical example to help. If you think of an electric fan which isn't switched on, you can see its propeller blades quite easily as they sit there, unused. Now imagine it is switched onto a very low speed, or low vibrational frequency. and starts to slowly whirr around. You can see the blades still but they are becoming blurred as they move. Then turn it to a higher speed and they become even more blurred. Turn it high enough and you can't even distinguish the blades anymore. This is how our own energies work in our aura. The faster they whirl, the less we can see: that is, until we become more attuned.

Other 'living' objects such as vegetables, fruit, plants and trees have auras too. Now try an experiment to practise seeing their aura. Take any live object (a household plant may be the easiest to begin with), place it against a plain, dark background and then shine a plain-coloured light onto it. As you did with the palm exercise, try to breathe slowly and regularly and focus your eyes on the object itself. Try not to stare intently, but let your gaze soften as much as possible, rather as though you were trying to see a 3-D picture. After a while, you may start to see a hazy glow, or cloud, around the edges of the object. It will probably appear colourless to you but have a luminous quality, a little as though you were staring into a candle's flame. This is the object's energy. Don't worry if you don't see anything initially. You may need to be tuned in through the exercises before you can open up enough to this new phenomenon.

It gets even more interesting when you know that even inanimate, i.e. non-living, objects all have an aura too! But their energy is placed onto and into them by other living objects with which they come into contact. This is important for you to understand when we come to the chapter on psychometry. Obviously this energy is finer and can be infinitely more confusing because one object may be handled by a wealth of different people. Think of the aura of a coin as it's handled by countless people!

Fascinating in-roads have been made into the study of the aura, particularly in recent years. For instance, Kirlian photography is actually the means of photographing the energy field, usually around the hands. A black and white photograph is developed, and can then be used as a diagnostic tool to help someone learn more about themselves. You can now also have your head's aura photographed in colour and if you attend a large psychic or spiritual exhibition, you will possibly see this being offered.

For now, you need to start becoming aware of your own aura. As previously mentioned, our aura constantly changes and fluctuates according to our moods and environment, and as you start developing your psychic abilities, your aura will expand. You therefore have to learn how to contract it again and protect yourself. If you don't, you can leave yourself very vulnerable to other people's unwanted influences.

So practise becoming aware of your own aura. Do you hate getting into crowded trains or lifts? No wonder, with all those auras squashed together! Or notice how, even if a person you like steps too close to you, you want to take a few steps away. They've intruded into your aura and it makes you feel uncomfortable. Have you noticed how different spaces have different auras? One room in a house has a completely different feel from another, especially different bedrooms. Different situations make our auras expand and contract. Can you think of examples when this would happen? Try to notice on a day-to-day basis when you feel your aura has grown or shrunk and why.

If you have chosen to work with a partner, or if you have a willing friend or relative, you can practise feeling another person's aura. Ask your volunteer to stand comfortably in the middle of a room, away from furniture and walls, with their hands loosely by their sides. Ask them to keep their eyes open throughout the experiment, as they might feel dizzy or offbalance otherwise. Now you are going to practise feeling their aura. Remember to breathe regularly and deeply before you start. When you feel reasonably relaxed, start moving your hands around them, starting at least two or three feet away from their physical body. Aim your hands towards their solar plexus area, not at their heart or around their head. Do keep your distance to begin with, and then gradually, very gradually, move your hands further in towards them. At what point do you naturally want to stop? Some people's aura will extend over three feet from their body, others less. If you are relaxed and breathing properly, you should feel a somewhat marshmallow-like texture where their aura begins and you should naturally want to stop and not penetrate their aura further. (This is also a useful exercise to increase your feelings of sensitivity and respect towards your sitter). Once you can feel something, move your hands over the rest of their aura. When does it get hotter suddenly? Or colder? Do you feel a sudden pull towards an area and then feel you should move further away from others? Don't spend any time around the heart chakra or over the crown of the head; just pass over those areas lightly. Once you have explored their aura, ask your volunteer what it felt like for them. Did they have any feelings of hot or cold, or any uncomfortable or comforting sensations? The more you practise this exercise, preferably with more than one volunteer, the more you will become attuned to auras and appreciate how they are all so different.

What you cannot do is make your aura disappear completely. It is a mostly invisible, relentless friend that accompanies you everywhere, constantly changing as you change. There is a theory that we only lose our aura a few moments before we pass over to the other side. There is a particularly spine-chilling 'story' about a highly developed psychic who was about to step into a crowded lift that was making its way down to the ground level. She was suddenly aware that no person in the lift had an aura and, stunned and confused, she hastily stepped out again. The lift then crashed through to ground level, killing all occupants. It's a horrible story but it's been included because it powerfully demonstrates the sort of level at which psychics can work.

In psychic work, you do use energies from your own aura in activating your chakras but what is vital is that you also draw in the pure white light, the universal energy, as well. As you 'give out' through your psychic work so must you repeatedly renew your energies. This constant flow of energy is essential for psychic development and for your own wellbeing. So often inexperienced healers and psychics make the mistake of using only their own energies to help others. They soon end up exhausted and, in some cases, extremely ill.

Now, apart from the pure universal energy, there is one other form of energy which we also use in psychic work and this is what we call the earth's energy. This we draw up through our base chakra from the ground, again using exercises detailed in the next chapter. The purpose of this energy is to literally 'ground' us and keep us in touch with reality and our roots. This is especially important for beginners in psychic work because as you'll soon discover, once you start tuning in and drawing in the universal energy, it can be a very 'heady' experience! It's a great way to 'fly away with the fairies' and although it can be very pleasant, it won't help you in psychic development unless you also have the earth's energy to keep you solid and focused. This is often visualised as a gold or pink light coming into you through the soles of your feet, although it can be a colour of your own choice, so long as it's not a dark, heavy colour and it doesn't conflict with any of the seven major chakras' colours.

Once you understand how many energies we have spinning all around us, you'll also begin to realise that we have to 'balance' all these out somehow within us. We've got universal and earth energies and our own energies from our own aura all whirring madly inside and we have to learn to control and balance them. It might help you to now think of your body with masses of electrical currents flowing around and through you. These currents are known as 'nadis' and ancient yogis considered there to be more than 72,000 nadis connected to each body. However, just as we don't need to know every minor chakra in our body, only the seven main ones, so we will simply concentrate on the three main 'nadis' or meridians. They are:

1 The Sushumna – this is the main nadi and runs vertically through the spine, connecting all seven chakras.
2 The Ida – to the left of our brain, controlling the female part of us, also depicted as the moon.
3 The Pingala – to the right of our brain, controlling the masculine part of us, often depicted as the sun.

The Ida and Pingala both spiral around the Sushumna. It might clarify the image for you if you can visualise a holy cross, then see the Sushumna as the upright section and both the Ida and the Pingala as spirals of energy coming from the outside of the cross-bar and weaving through the Sushumna. Take a moment to create that in your mind. Very often, these three major nadis aren't balanced within us, which is hardly surprising when you consider how much is happening in and around our body! Chapter Five details a very simple exercise that will balance these energies and further your psychic development. When our nadis are properly aligned and the energy can flow, unhindered, this is known as awakening our 'Kundalini'. This is a very powerful cosmic energy that mostly lies inactive in our system and it's located at the base of the Sushumna in the base chakra. Because it is such a powerful force, we need to treat it with respect.

Before we start our tuning-in process, a word of warning. Once you start 'opening up' it will leave you in exactly that sort of state: very 'open' to everything around you. This can be wonderful. It can also be off-putting as there are many energies out there in the world and some are not so nice as others. To begin with, you may not be able to choose which influences you allow in and this means that another essential part of your training is to learn the 'cleansing process', followed by the 'closing down' process: the means whereby you let go of all the outside influences which you have accumulated and then protect yourself again for the everyday world. Not only is this vital in psychic work, it can be a wonderful help and comfort in your day-to-day life as well.

So, before starting the next chapter, please make sure you are clear about the following points:

1 What the aura is, how we use it in psychic work and how we need to start becoming aware of our own auras.
2 The importance of using the universal and the earth energy.
3 The three main 'nadis', where they are and their functions.
4 Our vulnerability whilst we are 'tuned in' and the importance of learning the cleansing and closing down processes.

Chapter 4:
'TUNING IN'

Now you're ready to start! It's suggested you read through this chapter several times before you actually put the exercises into practice, particularly if you've opted to do this work on your own, without a partner. You need to memorise the exercises because having to stop half-way through to frantically check which bit comes next will severely disrupt your powers of concentration. If you're now working with a partner, one of you can opt to read the other person through the whole process and then you can swap over. Decide which you want to do.

Opening up

The first thing to ensure is that you have a comfortable, completely private and mostly quiet space where you will not be interrupted. Put the answerphone on and make sure no children, animals or adults will come rushing through half-way into your work. If you have a room which locks, so much the better, provided no one is claustrophobic. A comfortable temperature will help, too. It's hard to concentrate if you're feeling very cold or extremely hot. Soft illumination is preferable to harsh lighting. Strong perfume can also be distracting.

Once you're satisfied with the ambience, choose a comfortable chair in which to sit. A soft armchair is not recommended: many people can relax so much they drift off completely when they're beginners! Conversely, a really hard upright can make any level of relaxation difficult. A lightly padded chair of average height will help you most.

Sit comfortably into the chair, with your legs uncrossed and your feet flat on the floor. Take off your shoes if it's more comfortable and loosen any restrictive clothing. It's always best to wear loose, soft garments if you can. Relax your arms and let your hands fall loosely in your lap, preferably not touching one another. Settle your weight into the seat, becoming aware of how heavy you feel in the chair.

When you feel reasonably relaxed, start to concentrate on your breathing. Become aware of each intake of breath and how it caresses the inside of your body. Enjoy the release as you exhale. Start noticing the rhythm of your breathing and how soothing it is. If you feel any aches or twinges in your body, take a breath in and try to send that breath to the spot which is hurting and use it to disperse the discomfort. As you breathe out, take the ache with it and release it out into the distance. Feel your rib cage expand with each breath and enjoy the sense of freedom it allows. Try not to raise your shoulders as you breathe but let them feel heavy and relaxed.

Once you feel in tune with your breathing and completely relaxed, start to visualise a beautiful, pure, bright, white light streaming into the centre of the room from above you. Feel the warmth and brightness of it, let it become as strong and powerful as you want, streaming in endlessly. It's there, always there and by visualising it you make it stronger all the time. Wait until you know it is there, until you can sense its intensity, then allow the light to come closer, to come down into the room and to circle round you, all the way around you. Fill the whole room with that beautiful light energy. Feel yourself bathed by its warm glow and enjoy the sensation. Initially, it may take you a while to do this but once you have felt this white energy, knowing it is there allows you to connect with it immediately and it truly will become an easy part of the process.

Then visualise this pure white light coming down through the top of your head through the crown chakra. This is a chakra that's always open, remember, so you can just let the light enter into you and slowly filter through your body, gently cleansing and rejuvenating every part of you, releasing aches and pains. Let the light trickle through you like a warm shower: through your head, neck, shoulders, arms, hands and then let it run out through your fingers. Then on through the rest of your body: chest, rib cage, stomach, all through the vertebrae of your back, then through your hips, legs, down into your feet and then again let it filter out through your toes, taking any tension or worries with it. Repeat this process several times, enjoying the sensation of muscles and joints relaxing, of cares and problems washing out of you, feeling refreshed as the pure white light cleanses and purifies. Always bring in the light as you breathe in and feel the tension trickling out through fingers and toes on each exhalation of breath. Take as long as you want with this section until you feel content to move on to the next.

Now concentrate on your feet as they rest on the floor. Make sure they feel heavy and weighted. If it helps, imagine the soles of your feet with roots attaching them down into the ground, feeling secure and safe. Then visualise the earth energy coming up through the ground and into the soles of your feet. Use pink or gold as a colour or a colour that feels right to you, avoiding the chakras' rainbow colours and any dark, heavy colours. Stretch your toes and feel this earth energy coming through into them. Remember to use your breathing to help the visualisation and with each breath in, slowly draw the energy up through your body. Take plenty of time to fill every space within you; don't rush the process. Think of each part of your body, each muscle and joint and work your way up the body through to your shoulders. Then let the earth energy flow down your arms and hands and out through your fingers. Then back to the shoulders and up your neck and into your head, feeling it meet the pure white light at your crown and blend with it.

Now you are experiencing the flow of the universal energy and the earth energy, you are ready to open your chakras. Start with the first, the base chakra, located at the bottom of your spine. Remember it opens downwards to the ground and it is always open although we need to speed it up, or open it more fully. This sensation of opening will be different for everybody and you can use different visualisation techniques to help you. Imagine it is an electric fan that has been turning very slowly but you are turning up the speed. Imagine the petals of a beautiful flower unfolding. Picture a drawbridge or a door slowly opening or a parcel being unwrapped – or use another image that works for you. The chakra is about three inches from your physical body and as it opens, everybody will experience a different sensation. Some describe it as a flutter like butterfly wings, others a tingle, some a warmth, or a twirling sensation. In the beginning you may feel nothing. Whatever you feel is right for you. If at any time whilst opening the chakras you feel uncomfortable, simply use the light to cleanse yourself through. Cleanse yourself as often as you like. The base chakra is red so as you open the centre, imagine the colour red. Don't just think of the colour, imagine it all around you and in you, feel the colour, feel its richness and vibration. Use a symbol if it helps you to think of the colour. Think of a red apple, or a red poppy – or a red postbox! Use anything that means red to you. Feel the colour red entering your base chakra and filling you with red. Wait until you feel happy with that image before moving on.

Now move up to the second chakra which is the solar plexus, located near your navel. This opens front and back so you need to imagine two centres opening. Use your own thought process to make it 'open' for you. Then think of the colour orange and fill yourself with it. Again use anything you like to help you feel that colour: a juicy orange, a carrot, or even your favourite orange sweater – whatever you like. Remember to open front and back to let two lots of colour come in and fill you. Are you also remembering to keep breathing?

Then concentrate on the spleen, which is above and to the left of the navel. This also opens front and back, so use your preferred method of visualisation to open it. In the beginning, try a different thought process each time and then discover what is most powerful for you. This is yellow, so try to fill yourself with that wonderful, warm colour. Picture the bright sun, or a field full of yellow rapeseed, or a pretty sunflower – or a lemon or banana! Let the colour yellow enter you front and back and fill you with its richness.

Now we move to the heart chakra, above the chest in the middle. Open its drawbridge or petals or switch on the fan and start opening the heart's energy centre, front and back. You may find the sensation of opening start to change here. It's very hard to describe until you experience it for yourself but you are now moving onto a higher vibration and the feeling may be finer or start to tingle in a faster sensation. If you feel nothing different, don't dwell on that, just continue opening up. The colour is now green, so picture a golf course, or an evergreen tree, or a lime, or any green vegetable. Experiment to find what best symbolises green to you. Once you can see the colour clearly, draw it into your heart centre both front and back and let that warm, loving colour fill you completely. When you feel filled with the green light of love and compassion, move on.

Next is the throat and its chakra is at the hollow of the throat. Front and back, open the centres and experience your own tingle or whirring or butterfly tickle. As we move higher, it will become lighter and finer still. Then tune in to the colour of sky blue. It's usually easiest to imagine a cloudless sky but if something else suits you – a calm blue sea, for example – that's fine too. Let the cooling, inspirational colour of sky blue now come into your body, front and back, and fill every part of you.

Then make your way up your body to your third eye, in the middle of your forehead. This also opens front and back, so start your process of opening, again always remembering to keep breathing. It's very easy to stop altogether for a moment as you concentrate on opening and creating colours, so keep checking that you are letting your body breathe all the time. None of this has to be rushed; everybody works in their own time, so at this stage it doesn't matter how quickly or slowly the process works for you. The third eye energy centre is purple, so what symbolises purple for you? A violet, perhaps? Or a purple plum? Create your own image and then breathe it in through the front and back, taking the vibrant colour purple down and through your entire body, feeling it wash over you as you become that colour.

Now focus on your crown chakra and open it further. Remember this centre, like the base, is always open but we need to open it further. Open those flower petals or that door or increase the whirring fan's speed. This centre opens downwards into the body, so once it feels open, pull the white light down through your entire body again, feeling the pure energy infiltrating every tiny part of your body. Allow yourself to really feel every part of you being energised and refreshed by this.

If you feel heady or off-balance, or 'away with the fairies', you need to concentrate your energies back to earth. To do this, think only of your feet and concentrate all your energies on them. Imagine long, deep roots growing out of the base of your feet and anchoring you deep into the ground. Feel how heavy your feet are and think of the floor and how it feels under you. Spend as much time as you like thinking about your feet and the earth before you open your eyes.

Now you are open and ready to work!

HOWEVER, BEFORE DOING THIS YOU MUST FIRST PRACTISE THE CLEANSING AND CLOSING DOWN PROCESSES. THIS IS MOST IMPORTANT.

You've read earlier why this is necessary because at any time during initial psychic work you may feel uncomfortable or you might pick up on someone else's discomfort and take on board their symptoms for a while. This is harmless,

AS LONG AS YOU CLEANSE AND RE-ENERGISE.

If you have opened up properly, you will understand why this is important. You will probably feel very good, still slightly 'up in the air' and extremely aware of everything around you. The room may appear much brighter, richer; it may even have a resonance you weren't aware of before; all your senses feel heightened and sharpened. All this is wonderful: congratulations! Allow yourself a moment to acknowledge what you have accomplished before you close your eyes again and start the cleansing process.

Cleansing

Before you close down all the chakras, you need to ensure you are not leaving anything unwelcome inside you. Once you start working properly with others, you will be pulling outside influences into your own aura. You have to do this to enable you to 'read' your subject and use your psychic abilities. So let's practise getting rid of those effects.

Again, you use the bright white light coming through the top of your crown chakra and feel it wash all through you – but this time be aware of any residue you may still have inside. Did something you pick up disturb you, unbalance you, cause mild pain or emotional hurt somewhere? You must be aware of your own body, tune in to what it is saying, and then consciously let every bit go. As you breathe in the white light, direct it to wherever you feel off-balance (quite often it's around the solar plexus and spleen areas, our emotional centres) and really concentrate on washing the feeling away.

Another image that may help you more than simply using the white light, is to imagine the white light as a cool, comforting waterfall and actually feel the water trickling into your body and through your whole system, giving you a good psychic wash inside! Once you've practised this a few times, it again becomes an easy part of the process. Even create your own waterfall in some idyllic naturalistic setting within your own mind and picture yourself actually stepping under the waterfall as you do so. Or do you have a dream of the perfect shower in a perfect bathroom? Create whatever stimulates your imagination and makes you feel really good and then put yourself within that picture. The stronger and more vivid your picture, the more comforting and healing the cleansing process becomes. Always remember to let the residue water or light spill out of your fingers and toes, never leave any inside you. Inhale the light or waterfall and release through the fingers and toes on the exhalation.

This cleaning and purifying technique is also wonderfully useful for everyday life. You know when you step off a crowded, smelly train, having felt almost suffocated by everyone else's aura? Take a moment to 'cleanse' then. Once you've practised a lot, you'll even be able to do it as you walk out of the station. Your own image of the light or waterfall or shower will be so strong for you that you can conjure it up anywhere, anytime. Even use it while you're actually squashed in the train! Create your own psychic space and step into the waterfall. The joy of your own imagination is that no one else knows what you're doing. There are so many times in our everyday life when outside stress comes crowding in on us: visiting a sick friend or relative, communicating with a bad-tempered person, dealing with a client at work who is being very demanding, being stuck in a traffic jam, or coping with nerves and feeling sick before facing a daunting project. On all these occasions, cleansing your body and aura is an invaluable tool to help you cope. The more you practise it, the more powerful a tool it will become.

Closing down

This is as important as the cleansing process because unless you protect your aura as you finish psychic work, you will continue, even unconsciously, to pick up further energies from people. Don't start this process until you have cleansed properly.

Once you feel psychically 'scrubbed clean', become aware of how your aura has expanded during your opening up process. If you have been practising aura awareness through everyday life, you'll be able to sense how much wider it feels now. You need to contract it again. Concentrate first of all and think how large it feels. Where are its outer edges: three, four, five feet away? Wider than that? Work out how far away it is and then slowly pull it back towards you. As you take in a breath, feel it suck inwards, closer to you. Once it feels comfortable around you, stop.

Now you need to go through the chakras, one by one, closing each down. You don't need to use the colours for this shutting down process.

Again, start with the base chakra and concentrate on its location at the base of the spine. This one is always open but we've revved it up to spin much faster than normal so now we have to slow it down. Use the reverse process of what you used before: fold up all the flower petals until they close into each other, pull up the drawbridge, close the door, or turn the fan down to low. Depending on how well you opened in the first place, i.e. how fast your energy centre is spinning, it may take a few moments for you to control its speed and slow it down. You must always be in control during psychic work, so practise that control now by making the chakra spin more slowly. Once you are satisfied that it really has slowed down, then psychically 'seal' the centre with a circle of light and a cross. It might help if you imagine a psychic pen which has a nib of pure light instead of an inky tip. Use that pen to draw a circle and then a cross.

Then work your way up the chakras. Can you now remember their order? You see why it's one section you really need to memorise. Base, solar plexus, spleen, heart, throat, third eye and crown. Use the same process but remember the next five must all be closed completely. This may make it easier for you; imagine the centres utterly still and closed, sealed with a circle and a cross. The crown, like the base, is always open but because it will have opened much more during your work, you must take time to slow it down. Again, don't rush this process. Take your time.

If, once you have closed all seven chakras, you still feel a little 'out of it', cleanse again with the white light or your waterfall. You can never cleanse too much! If you don't feel grounded properly, again use your feet anchored to the floor as your guide. Imagine them with long, strong roots into the ground and feel how heavy they are. After a few minutes, your energies should be well grounded again.

As a last protective measure, you should draw a psychic 'cloak' up around you to make you feel secure and safe. Again, there are various ways of doing this. Some like to see it as a sheath of warm light coming up and around them; others use an image of fabric (try something soft like wool or silk which feels good against your skin and always use a light colour, not a dark one); some imagine an enormous, warm fluffy towel enveloping them with security. Use your own image, but make sure the colour you use is a light one, not dark. A dark one could leave you feeling low in energy, as dark colours absorb the light. It might help you to imagine the cloak coming up from your feet and gradually coming up over your whole body as high as your neck. If you still feel 'open', then use a zipper or buttons or velcro to do up the front and/or back to make you feel even more secure. Experiment with what feels right for you. If you feel too bottled up, release the psychic fabric a bit. Everyone feels differently about this protection, so tune in to what suits you.

If you are working with another person, make sure you give them the space to create what works for them. Chances are you will both have very different images for opening and closing chakras, visualising colours, cleansing and protecting yourself. By all means, discuss your various images but never try to impose your methods on someone else.

A final word about opening and closing down. As a beginner, never practise 'opening up' in public and in unprotected environments but feel free to practise closing down at absolutely any time. The reason for this is that we can open up quite easily under certain circumstances and not realise it. A sudden rush of love can open our heart chakra or an impassioned speech will open our throat centre, but we very rarely think of closing ourselves off again. Also, when you do start working with your psychic abilities, it is very exciting and the natural urge is to want to share your discoveries with others. That's wonderful, of course, but even by animatedly talking to friends about what we have done, we can start opening the chakras, without our consciously being aware. When we finish talking about it, we need to close down again. So, at this stage, only consciously open up under safe, controlled circumstances but practise closing down at any time.

Chapter 5:
BALANCING AND EXPANDING EXERCISES

Now you've learnt how to 'open' and 'cleanse' and 'close', there are other exercises which will increase your psychic abilities. Again, read these through before following them.

Expanding your aura

As you've already read, your aura will expand as you practise psychic work but you can also use a technique to help you. This can be done either before or after opening up but you may find it more effective during the latter. Make sure your breathing is deep and regular. Closing your eyes will also help your concentration. Tune in to your own aura and feel it pulsating all around you, visualising its size and shape. Then start to 'see' it increasing in size that so that as you breathe in your aura puffs up. It's rather like pumping up a blow-up doll! – except our psychic body is being blown up with pure white energy, increasing our powers to work. Feel your aura reaching outwards to the walls of the room. Make it as large as feels comfortable; if it can fill the room and it feels good, that's fine. Keep expanding until you either can't increase it or it feels uncomfortable. If you feel discomfort, contract the aura inwards and use your cleansing technique to refresh you. Don't forget that an important part of the closing down process is the retracting of your aura.

Balancing your energies

If you remember from an earlier chapter, balancing our male and female energies (the Pingala and the Ida) around our main vertical meridian (the Sushumna) will also help increase our psychic abilities. This is a simple exercise which will balance you. It feels odd initially and looks even odder, so if you're practising with a friend, you may burst into laughter the first time you do this. It may look complicated as you read it, but as soon as you put it into practice, you realise it's easy to co-ordinate. The exercise is explained using your right hand but it's just as effective with your left. Try one and then the other to choose the best for you. Often the hand you write with is the easiest to use.

Also, if you have a cold or sinus trouble (such as asthma or hay fever), you'll have trouble with this exercise. You're advised to leave it until both nostrils are reasonably clear.

Place your hand, palm and fingers open, over your face, with the palm side against your face. Now place your thumb lightly over your right nostril so you can close off that nostril in a moment. Then bend your fourth finger (or ring finger) so that it can close off your left nostril. Where you place your index and third finger is optional but a good location is lightly over your forehead as it will then connect with your third eye chakra. Then what you need to do is lightly close your right nostril and breathe in through your left only for a count of four. Then close off your left nostril with your ring finger so that both nostrils are completely closed and hold for the count of four. Then release the thumb over your right nostril and breathe out through your right only for a further count of four. Then breathe in again through that same nostril, the right one, for a count of four. Close your right nostril with your thumb so both nostrils are closed and hold for four. Then open your left nostril and breathe out for four. Repeat the whole process several times.

Initially, you may feel dizzy or short of breath. If you do, stop, sit comfortably and ground yourself again by feeling your weight in the chair and the heaviness of your feet on the floor. When you feel ready, start again, but count only to two on each section and then gradually build up to four. Just a few repetitions of this exercise will leave you feeling very different. You'll know immediately that something has shifted within you although you may find it difficult to explain exactly what. Anytime you feel light-headed, remember to use the method of concentrating on your feet flat against the floor until you feel grounded again.

Lifting and lowering your energies through your chakras

This is rather like using your energies as a lift as you practise whooshing them up and down through the chakras. If you imagine each chakra is a floor level and your lift full of energy is whizzing up and down between the floors, you'll get some idea of what we need to accomplish! A highly experienced psychic can literally work at supersonic speed; in the time it takes you to snap your fingers, they will have opened all chakras and taken the energy level straight up to their crown, ready to stay there for further work. It will take you a while to reach that level. As already mentioned, with the psychic work detailed in this book we're only going as far as the fourth level: the heart chakra. So you need to practise this lifting and lowering of energies as the more proficient your 'lift' the faster you can work and the more psychic information you will receive.

Once you have finished the opening up exercises detailed in the previous chapter, your energies will have settled back at your base chakra. This is important to ground you before continuing. Now you can practise the sensation of raising that energy.

First of all try to lift it only as far as the second chakra, the solar plexus. Remember its location is near the navel. It may take you a while to experience this feeling, so try to picture your body as a lift and see the base chakra as ground level. You then have to draw in the energy to whoosh you up to the first floor. If you whisk it up as you inhale it will help your image. A word of warning: some people find this an easy task and can instantly bypass all the floors, shooting straight to the top! But at this stage, they will then immediately lose the energy as they plummet down again through the floors. If this happens to you, don't worry; it's a natural part of the learning process. This lifting and lowering is all about us being in control of psychic work and the control doesn't happen immediately. Try to make yourself the lift operator in control of all the buttons and make it clear that to begin with you want to stop at the first floor. After some practice, you should be able to raise the energy to the solar plexus chakra. Then you have to keep it there. You'll soon realise it wants to slip down again! So you need to keep drawing in the energy to maintain that level. Work only between the base and chakra to start off with, then when you feel ready lift the energy as far as the spleen. Again, you will find once you do this, you will most likely slip down the chakras again. Concentrate and remember to keep breathing to help you stay in control. Go as far as the heart chakra and then stop. At this stage, you'll find it hard enough to maintain control even at that level. Once you start to actively work with somebody else to give your 'readings' of them, you will discover that as soon as you receive a piece of information and then start to speak, your energy level will immediately drop down through the chakras. This is why you need to practise your 'lift' work to get used to constantly drawing energy up again, as this will enable you to keep receiving information during a sitting.

Chapter 6:
CHOOSING A 'SITTER' AND HOW TO TREAT THEM

Now you've reached the stage when you can start practising, so your next step is to find someone on whom you can practise! If you've been opting to work alone so far, this is when you need to find a friend or relative who is happy to be your guinea pig. The reason for this is that it's very difficult to practise psychic development on yourself. You need another person whom you can 'read' or 'tune into' and therefore increase your psychic potential. The best person is someone about whom you don't know a great deal, as you then can't be tempted to fall back on the safety of talking about aspects of their life with which you are already familiar. To clarify, if you choose someone you know well, then you won't know if the information you're receiving about them is truly psychic, or whether you are simply delving into your own personal knowledge of them.

You may feel daunted by the thought of working with someone you don't know well but it actually puts less pressure on you to prove yourself with a stranger, rather than a close friend. You may also wonder how you could possibly find someone suitable but it isn't as difficult as it sounds. Once you start talking to other people about wanting to increase your psychic abilities, you'll discover almost everyone has some interest in the phenomenon. Some may think they know it all already (they are always the people who know the least!) and some will be more cynical than others but most people will be intrigued. Indifference is rare in this field. If you can find the confidence to talk about your work to friends of a friend, or a relative's friend, you will start to discover quite a few people who say they're happy to be experimented upon! Of course, the logistics of mutual time and a suitable meeting place can narrow down the field. Also, you need to stress to your prospective sitter that as a beginner you can't guarantee positive results. You need to have the space to practise and make mistakes and keep trying. It's also counter-productive if you rush the opening-up process when you first start. So be honest with people from the beginning and it will make it easier for both of you. It's also important that you appreciate and acknowledge the time they are giving you: when someone feels appreciated, they become even more willing to bear with you as you work your way through the early stages.

Sitters who come to you for the first time probably won't really know what is going to happen and chances are they will be somewhat apprehensive. It's up to you to put them at their ease. The more relaxed they are, the easier it will be for you to pick up information. Make sure they are seated in a comfortable chair and check they're not too hot or cold or thirsty. All those factors affect the atmosphere in the room. Then explain to them what you're going to do. Explain that you take a few minutes to tune in by sitting quietly and concentrating on your breathing. Also remind them that it is only experimental and you can't guarantee results but you hope you will provide something useful. Explain you will start to speak as you sense or see things and ask them to respond mainly with a 'yes' or 'no'. They may be anxious to tell you about themselves but if they do, it lowers your ability to pick things up for yourself. Explain this to them and ask them to keep detailed comments to themselves until the end of the sitting when you have finished giving your information. Also let them know they don't have to be thinking or trying to 'give out' anything to you. It's a common mistake for people to make, putting psychic work into the realms of telepathy or ESP. You are tuning in to them and they don't have to do a thing, apart from relax as much as possible. Always, either at the beginning or end (or both), thank them for their assistance.

Once you have experimented with a few people, you really will appreciate how very different all human beings are: some will be very closed and hard to penetrate; others will seem to have information pouring out of them; some will fill you with a warm glow as you interpenetrate their aura; others will throw you off-balance. It's a fascinating process as you discover how truly individual we all are. Psychic work allows us concrete proof of that.

Now a few words about your responsibilities to your sitter. When you first start receiving information psychically, it is incredibly exciting and almost impossible not to immediately tell them everything you are seeing and sensing. However, you must give consideration to the way you say everything; always stop to think what you're going to say before you say it. Here are a few examples to demonstrate why this is so necessary:

1 You've tuned in to your sitter and suddenly, after a few moments of nothing, an image flashes across your mind. You're thrilled, of course: something is happening! You say quickly, 'A coffin. I see a coffin.' Can you imagine what that image might mean to your sitter? They may have a friend or relative who's ill and immediately assume they're now going to die. Or they themselves may have a terrible fear of death (many people do) and think they're about to die. To you, the coffin may have seemed perfectly innocent, covered in pretty flowers perhaps, and your image may have been a pleasant one. Maybe it symbolically represents the person having let go of a problem or saying good-bye to an unhappy relationship – *but you just said 'a coffin'*.

2 You've tuned in and suddenly feel a twinge in your stomach and say 'There's something wrong in your stomach

area. I sense a pain there'. The way most people are programmed is to fear the worst: an illness (often cancer), an operation, something terrible that will adversely affect their lives. That pain you picked up on might have been an emotional one: perhaps the person feels as if they are emotionally being 'kicked in the gut' by someone at present, or perhaps they are very worried about an upcoming project at work, or maybe they just have butterflies in their stomach from the nervousness of being one of your first sitters – *but you just said 'something's wrong with your stomach'.*

3 You've tuned in and picked up on your sitter's concern about their mother. You say 'Your mother's unwell and you're worried about her'. They might then think you're implying her condition will worsen or they might even say that it's true but her problem isn't serious. You think nothing of it and carry on. Then your sitter returns home to discover an answerphone message from their father (who never phones them normally) asking them to ring as soon as possible. Your sitter naturally assumes something has happened to their mother and has a distressing time until they get hold of their father and discover he only wanted them to video a television programme for him! *You added to their stress by your casual remark, 'your mother's unwell'.*

You might think it highly unlikely you'd ever be as insensitive as the three examples above but the truth is you will probably be even more so, *unless you stop and think first.* It is hard when you're excited to consider your phraseology but it's one of your most important jobs. Going back to the examples above, here's how you could have phrased things to avoid alarm:

1 It's never wise to mention symbols such as a coffin, gun or knife – or any object which might be construed as threaten-

ing – because people won't understand its meaning unless you elaborate. Instead, ask yourself what the symbol is 'saying' to you and then phrase your sentence something like: 'I feel something or someone was troubling you but you have now let it go' or 'I feel as if something has been stabbing you in the back recently and you want to do something about it' or 'I feel that someone may be shooting down your confidence right now and you want to deal with that'. There is a wealth of ways to interpret the symbols you receive but this analysis can only come with practice and until you can work with it and understand it, be extremely careful about your words. If you are in doubt about the images, don't mention any potentially distressing objects, just cleanse yourself and move on to the next image.

2 Physical pains are tricky but if you feel whatever you pick up is on the physical and not emotional level, then phrase your comments something like this: 'Have you had a slight tummy upset recently, like indigestion?' If they offer a 'yes' response or admit to something similar, then cleanse yourself of the feeling before moving on. If you feel it may not be a physical pain but a related emotional response, then try to tune in on that level and offer a related comment such as 'I think you have a gut feeling that someone around you isn't treating you properly and you want to rectify that' or 'I feel you're very nervous about some ongoing project in your life'.

3 If you feel you can offer some concrete advice or help about their mother being unwell, then do so. For instance, you might feel your sitter is worrying themself so much that they have got everything out of proportion or are making themselves ill over it; then you can advise them to slow down and find some time for themselves. Or you might see that they could do something more to help but they are holding back for some reason. Or they may be feeling guilty when they've no need to do so. Or they might be troubled by a lack of communication in their relationship with their mother which they see as a state of being unwell. You need to be clear about what you want to say before you speak. If all you can see is that their mother is unwell but get no further information, cleanse yourself and pass on. Unless you can offer something constructive and comforting, reporting negative images on their own doesn't offer help to anyone.

Also, make sure you always close the sitting with a positive statement. Your final words will be the most memorable and may stay with them for quite a while. It's so important that they are left feeling uplifted and not depressed. They are giving you their time, free of charge, and they deserve to have a pleasant experience as a result. (The added bonus is that it will also make them feel more inclined to sit for you again.) This does not mean you should ever lie to your sitter and exaggerate something simply to make it sound good. It just means you need to concentrate on the positive yourself. By all means do offer thought-provoking comments during the reading but never leave them in a confused or sad state. You should always check this before they leave because you might not realise that something you've said has worried or thrown them. Most people are much more sensitive than you first acknowledge but hurt, confusion, sadness and anger are often deeply buried emotions and you may not tap into those initially. When in doubt, ask them more than once if they have any more questions or if anything left them confused. Tell them no matter how silly it seems, to please ask you. Be honest and let them know that your job is to leave them in a calm and pleasant state and you want to know if you have succeeded. Hopefully, they will tell you they feel marvellous/ better/ more peaceful/ uplifted. If they offer any negative adjective, ask them what prompted that feeling and then clear it up before they go.

This responsibility for how we speak will crop up a great deal through this book, so please start thinking about it now. This is an area of psychic work that can spill over into your everyday life and benefit you in your own relationships. How often do we all really stop and think about what we say before we say it? – especially if we're angry or frustrated or very excited. It will help you a great deal if you start noticing how you speak normally at work and at home. If you rephrase certain comments or requests at work or with your family and friends, do they respond more favourably?

Chapter 7:
AURIC READING

When you have chosen your first 'sitter' – or rather, when you have chosen each other – then a good place for beginners to start is with an auric reading.

This is when you tune in to someone's aura to give you a reading of what is going on with that person in their present life, and it works on an emotional, feeling level. It will help if you understand that what you are doing in this process is tapping into your sitter's etheric level of the aura. If you remember, this is the first layer of the aura and deals with their present, physical life. This sort of reading can provide wonderfully accurate details but what it can't do is tell the sitter something they don't already know, although it may be something from their subconscious as well as their conscious state. It is literally you 'reading' the sitter from their aura and because every aura changes constantly what you receive will differ from day to day: even from hour to hour. However, auric reading is a very valuable starting point for psychics to learn how to work and to test their own accuracy.

Make sure your sitter is comfortably settled and that you have explained everything to them as detailed in the previous chapter. Then concentrate on yourself and go through the opening up process. Make sure you have practised this enough before your first experiment, so that you feel confident working through the various steps, sure of what is coming next without having to check in the book. The more you have gone through the procedure, the more easily and quickly you will be able to open yourself up. It isn't until you have your first sitter that you will fully understand how important this practising is for everyone. You can be very relaxed on your own, working through the exercises in peace and quiet, feeling calm and in control. That changes so quickly when someone else is suddenly sitting there, looking at you expectantly! Prepare yourself for the shock of your first sitting by allowing yourself to be nervous and admitting it to your sitter. They're probably just as nervous as you are, after all. Do wait until you feel balanced and open, before you start the auric reading.

To begin with, it may help if you lightly take the person's hand in yours, or place your hand lightly over one of theirs. This is a personal matter as, depending on how well you know the sitter, it may not be appropriate. It isn't necessary to increase communication; it's simply that as beginners we feel more reassured with the physical touch than with the psychic one. Sometimes, that physical touch can give us the added confidence we need. If touching is uncomfortable for either of you, then choose not to make that contact.

Remember, your breathing is all-important in your work and try to keep it even and deep. For this exercise, we need to bring the energies up as far as the spleen, so start using your psychic 'lift' and draw the energies in and up as far as the spleen. As soon as you start to speak, often before, the energy will drop again, so you must constantly renew, pushing the energy up again.

Once you feel you have drawn the energy as high as the spleen, then you have to give your energy out to the sitter's solar plexus area and then draw that energy back in again. In other words, you give out to them but you then draw their energies and aura back into your own. This is the mechanism that allows you to 'read' their aura and the process probably won't work for you immediately. Some of you may find the giving out and receiving back in again something you can create easily; for others, it may feel a bit like trying to get a rusty engine to work. For those who find it difficult, try using a visualisation technique to get the energy flowing back and forth. You could try seeing your solar plexus as full of tentacles that reach out and pull your sitter's aura back to you, or see a bulldozer's arm reaching out and coming back full of their aura for you! Or you might prefer to see it as a stream of light going from your aura, mixing with their aura, and then returning to you. Invent your own method that works for you. Once you start the energy flowing, then you need to keep a rhythm up. This spiral of energy (often referred to as egg-shaped because it arcs away from you and then returns to you in another arc) needs to be constant for you to receive information. Once you stop the breathing and let the energy drop you won't be able to pick up anything further.

It's advisable for you to keep your eyes closed, as this helps concentration. The first sensation you often need to embrace is one of feeling silly! Almost everyone feels this initially. You doubt your own ability and wonder what on earth you are doing with this person in a room, trying to sense – well, you aren't sure what you're trying to sense but it certainly feels stupid! Don't be put off by that emotion. Accept that you feel unsure because we all do in everything we first attempt, whether it's learning to ski or studying a new computer programme or even saying 'I love you' for the first time in a relationship. Once you allow yourself to feel silly, the feeling will slip away and you can proceed.

After that, various sensations may start to happen. If you get nothing at all, that is alright, too. Don't worry. Just keep breathing and keep the energy spiralling back and forth. Everyone works differently and it will take you a while to decide what is actually happening to you. You may only tune in to a coolness or heat from their aura and then not pick up anything more. That is a start! Congratulate yourself on that and keep breathing.

Every psychic works differently and has to find their own method of dealing with what they receive psychically: some only get symbols or images; some see only colours; some just feel and sense emotions; some have physical responses only; some may just hear music and songs! Most of you will have a jumbled mass of all the above until you can discipline yourself. Most images and sensations will come and go swiftly; some will tangle themselves into and on top of each other, making them hard to decipher. Then some of you will feel and get nothing. Literally nothing. This may mean that you are still feeling uncertain about psychic phenomena or that auric reading isn't a powerful medium for you; but then psychometry or healing may be a more suitable field for your vibrations. Only through experimenting will you know what works for you.

When you do get something, anything, say what comes into your mind – *always remembering your responsibility to your sitter.* Make sure you phrase appropriately. What becomes difficult now is not letting your own brain take over and decide to interpret everything for you. That is what first happens. Provided the image or sensation is not one which may worry your sitter, say exactly what you see or sense. Do not decide for yourself at this stage what it means.

For instance: if you see a body of water, say that you see a lake or sea or river or whatever and don't immediately decide what that means. Your own brain might go on to say to you 'They're going to travel over water,' or 'They like boating' but you have to learn to shut out your own thoughts. It's hard to do. The truth is that water can also relate to emotional states, so the water you're seeing could be a symbolic image: turbulent seas could mean a troubled mind, babbling whirlpools some confusion or a calm lake peace and joy in a present situation. Only when you completely shut out your own thoughts and interference will you be able to be accurate.

Your images usually won't make sense to you but they may make sense to your sitter, so say what you see, however trite or non-sensical it seems. You might get a plate of baked beans on toast in front of your eyes and think you can't mention something so unimportant; but if you did, you might discover they had that as their lunch! Find the confidence to say what you are getting and if they can't relate to it, don't worry at this stage. It's wonderful just to be opening up and starting your psychic work, so don't expect too much immediately.

Anytime you receive something which is unpleasant or uncomfortable, immediately cleanse before renewing your energy and continuing.

The speed with which images and sensations come and go can also be frustrating. This is because you aren't keeping the energy flowing in the spiral effect. Remember as soon as you speak, the energy drops – and so does the image. With practice, it becomes easier to keep the speech and energies working simultaneously.

Sometimes you may get a series of seemingly unrelated objects or a tableau and feel at a loss to understand the pictures. For example, you see a beautiful sunset, followed by a ring and then a large palm tree. To you that means nothing, of course, so you hesitate to list them all – but go ahead, find the courage to speak. You may then have your sitter tell you they were recently married at sunset under a palm tree! Of course, not all your images will be that accurate and you will find your own thoughts and influences creeping in time and again until you discipline yourself to shut them out.

One common problem is that your sitter may not always connect a thought or image at the time you offer it to them, but it may make sense later. You may see a little brown dog, for instance, and ask if they own a dog. They may say they've never owned a dog and don't even like them particularly! Then later, they realise that on their bus journey over to see you, a brown dog and his owner sat next to them for the whole journey. So what you saw was accurate, because the little dog left some of his energies within your sitter's aura even though they weren't aware of it at the time.

Be very wary of trying to predict or offer solutions to problems you may pick up on. This is another popular mistake inexperienced psychics make. You may see, for example, that your sitter is about to take their driving test and is desperate to pass it. You may 'see' them passing it, waving their certificate and smiling and so you say to them they will undoubtedly pass. You won't necessarily be right because what you were picking up on in their aura was their own intense desire to pass. They themselves have created the image of passing because they hope for it so much. Predicting the future is not possible during an auric reading and if you think you are doing so, you're probably picking up only on the sitter's own wants and desires.

As you run out of images or sensations, you will also feel the energies weaken. Sometimes it's rather like the sensation of hitting the ground level suddenly in a lift: a slight jolt as you return to earth. Always remember to cleanse as soon as you finish. Even as you ask the sitter for their response, practise flushing everything away with your psychic waterfall or pure white light. Keep doing it even as they're talking, provided you can concentrate on two things at once.

Now ask them for as much feed-back as you can. If you intend to do further sittings with them, don't encourage them to talk about situations and conditions unrelated to what you have mentioned; that way you'll have more to discover on a subsequent occasion. However, do discuss any images, colours, emotions that you picked up on earlier.

Some connections may make sense when you probe a little further. A colour you saw might simply be the colour their office is painted, or their bedroom. It's natural that this will be within their aura because they're surrounded by that colour for a large part of each day. You might have seen a sports car when they don't own a car themselves but perhaps that sports car belongs to a neighbour and is always parked outside, so they see it every morning as they head out of their front door. Perhaps you got the image of a child's photo on a desk but they say they've no photo on their desk either at home or at work. But they might sit opposite someone in an open-plan office whose desk holds their child's photo. Again, it will be an image firmly implanted in their subconscious and part of their aura.

These examples don't mean to imply that you should keep digging until you can justify every image or feeling you experienced. That just isn't possible, especially on your first few attempts, when you're likely to either pick up very little or let your own imagination creep in for you. The latter is often what happens when you start to panic.

When you first sit there, if nothing comes through quickly you start to imagine nothing will ever happen and then you start to worry that your sitter is fed-up or bored and you feel the pressure to 'perform'. Unless you can cleanse that panic away and keep breathing and spiralling the energy, what will happen next is that you'll let your own brain start to create things for you. After a few sessions, you'll feel the difference for yourself when this happens and you'll be able to control it.

Conversely, when you genuinely do start reading someone's aura, you are likely to have your own brain interfering with nagging doubts, telling you that you must be imagining it and that you're not really capable of this work etc. Again, you have to cleanse those doubts and continue working.

As most of you will be starting with this exercise, this is when you'll have the greatest problems with confidence and anxiety. Keeping those nerves under control is a very important part of your psychic development. You must be in control at all times, so practise that feeling of containment from your very first sitting. Refuse to let your nerves and doubts take over and discover a new strength in yourself by doing so. This is another example of psychic work being a powerful means of you being able to learn more about yourself.

Another element you will be dealing with as soon as you start sittings, is that some people are much more closed than others. We all have our own protective shell that we need in order to go through life and not be too vulnerable. Some people's shells are paper-thin and that makes it much easier for you to work with them. However, other people will have built up far thicker walls. You may occasionally work with someone who literally seems to have steel-plated armour all around them, followed by a six-foot thick brick wall. You then have a choice to make. You can try to help them open up a little by making an effort to relax them, by talking to them, offering them a non-alcoholic drink or suggesting a more comfortable chair. Or you can try to tune in to them on an emotional level to see if you can gain some understanding as to why they seem so 'closed'. You then may have the opportunity to help them on a more personal level. Or you can honestly say to them that you aren't picking anything up, apologise and possibly offer them another reading on another day.

What is important is that you phrase your comments carefully. For you to tell your sitter that they seem to be a very closed person, is likely only to close them up further and leave them feeling very unsettled as they go out through the door. Part of your responsibility in psychic work is always to have respect and consideration for your sitter and this is when you need a great deal of care. By all means mention to them that they have very good self-defence mechanisms and that they seem to be very capable of looking after themselves; in other words, find a positive way of discussing this plate of armour but be careful not to infer a problem on their behalf. Some people also need to have excellent self-protection, such as those who work in very vulnerable and potentially dangerous situations: police and mental health workers, for example. They need their own cloak of protection during working hours and they may unconsciously keep themselves covered once they finish work. For you to imply that they could open up more and drop their guard a little would be fundamentally hazardous for them.

You will also deal with some people whose aura may seem very uncomfortable to you. Not all people are happy and well adjusted and you will be able to see just how true that is as you work with your sitters. That is when you need to really practise your cleansing techniques and to keep ridding yourself of unwanted images. Everyone has lovely aspects of their personality but sometimes you have to dig a bit deeper to find them. This then becomes a real test for you, to keep cleansing and moving on, until you find aspects of them that you feel happy to discuss. Once you have given a sitting to someone who you found to be more challenging than others, always remember to cleanse thoroughly and then put an extra thick cloak of protection around yourself. Remember to make sure that you have finished your sitting on a positive note and that your sitter is left in a good frame of mind.

Chapter 8:
PSYCHOMETRY

Once you feel you have practised auric reading enough to give you a sense of how it feels to open up, control your energies, tune in and receive information, then you can go on to try the field of psychometry.

This is where you hold an object in your hand and tune in to its vibrations so that you can glean some history of the object and, ultimately, some insight into the person to whom that object belongs. You've already read that everything, living and inanimate, has its own aura. In the case of the inanimate, its vibrations are very much determined by the living objects which have surrounded and touched it. The name 'psychometry' was coined in 1842 by an eminent American physician and scientist, J. Rhodes Buchanan (1814-1899) who spent a large portion of his life studying what we now call psychic phenomena. He made the word psychometry from the Greek word 'psyche' meaning soul, and 'metron' meaning measure. Therefore you get 'soul-measuring' or 'measurement by the human soul'.

Choosing the right object to practise on is very important. You don't want to make it complicated for yourself by having to deal with an object that has a mixture of vibrations from a combination of people. You'll have your work cut out as it is just to tune in to one vibration! The ideal is an object which has been worn by or been close to someone for a period of time but without outside influences. Antique jewellery, keys and money aren't good choices, nor an object that was with somebody else for quite a while before being handed down to the sitter (as you would then get a mixed reading of the previous owner and the present one). Avoid stones and crystals, as they have strong vibrations of their own and may confuse you. Even something such as a watch that has recently been in the repairer's for a week could have the vibrations of the repair shop all over it. Imagine how confusing that could be with so many customers in and out of a shop. Be firm with your sitter about the object they want you to read and don't be afraid to ask questions if you're unsure. That will save both of you feeling disappointed.

Quite often a sitter may come with an object belonging to someone else, say a parent, who has recently passed over. They want you to tell them about their deceased parent. This isn't possible because a reading on the level you can give will only respond to the vibrations of that object. If their parent hasn't touched the object for a while, it will, in the meantime, have picked up other influences. Also, they won't necessarily know who else has been close to that object before their parent. You see how complicated it can become? Be honest and explain that is not the level on which you can work at present. To make contact with a deceased spirit requires full use of all your chakras and a degree of discipline which you haven't yet attained. Contact with spirit is not for beginners. However, psychometry is a fascinating field of its own as you will soon discover.

So what is a good object? If someone has been married for a while and bought the ring new from a jeweller's (not an antique one), then that's an excellent choice. As it's also a symbol of their love for their partner, you will probably be able to pick up a fair amount about that relationship from it. Jewellery, in general, is a popular choice for psychometry because certain items are worn permanently by people and therefore heavily imbued with 'them' – but always check if the item is an antique and how long they themselves have owned it. A newish pen that only your sitter has used would also be filled with their vibrations. A wallet is also a good choice. Likewise, an object they have made themselves would be suitable, or an object which has been near them in a room for a long period of time, provided it's not been handled by other people.

Obviously, you can read an object without anybody else being in the room but if your sitter is with you, you then have the advantage of passing on the information as soon as you receive it.

Psychometry requires the use of the chakras as far as the spleen, as in auric reading. So, as with an auric reading, you need to settle yourself comfortably, open up all your energy centres, let the white light in through your crown and let it wash over you, and then lift your energies up as high as the spleen. Once you feel in the right state to work, have your sitter hand you the object. Take it loosely in one hand and remember to keep breathing and lifting those energies to the spleen. You may find through practice that one hand is more sensitive than the other, or you may like to use both by cupping the object completely. Try variations and feel the difference of each.

Give yourself plenty of time to receive the messages and images. Some of you may be fortunate enough to tune in quickly but the majority need to take longer. Again, as with the auric reading, say exactly what you see and feel, always taking into account the suitability of what you are saying. You may find having a solid object in your hand gives you more confidence than trying to tap in to someone's aura. Use that confidence to express yourself clearly and always, as soon as you speak, remember to then re-new your energies.

Occasionally, you will read an object and nothing you say will make any sense to your sitter. You need courage to keep going under those circumstances but continue reporting what you see and feel for a few minutes and then, once they are sure they can't take on board any of what you are saying, let all those images go and cleanse yourself thoroughly. Then ask your sitter how long they have had the object and if they know who owned it before them. You will probably have tapped in to another owner whose personality was dominant, irrespective of how long ago they owned the object. Just as some people come across as more forceful and energetic than others, so objects respond accordingly. If your present sitter is very shy and retiring, lacking in confidence and energy, it's no wonder that the previous owner is still dominating the object. Ask your sitter if they have another object they could give you and if this isn't possible, perhaps you could offer them an auric reading so they don't feel they have wasted time in being with you.

If you are working with a friend and both of you try psychometry with the same object, you'll probably discover you each have a different reading to give on the same item. This is normal and not a cause for concern. One person may tap in to the sitter's emotional state and the other may pick up material objects which surround that person. It is interesting if you can work with someone else to get used to the differences and know that each reading is valid, but from a different perspective.

Something else that often happens in psychic work is the ability to get the complete opposite of something, especially in auric reading and psychometry. This is because people's dislikes create very strong emotions and those negative vibrations are easy to pick up on. You may see a cat, for instance, and say 'You are very fond of cats. Do you own a cat?' Their response? 'Oh no, I hate cats. Can't stand them.' This may happen quite a bit, so if you aren't sure of the emotion attached to what you are seeing, you could always phrase it something like this, 'I see a cat around you very strongly. I think you must either love cats or have a fear of them.' Fear is another very strong emotion that has an effect on our aura and objects next to us. For example, if someone has a great fear of knives, you are quite likely to pick up on that in their aura. Again, think before you comment on an image like that. If in doubt, don't comment but cleanse yourself and move on.

You can also practise psychometry on your own. The next

time you receive a letter that you don't recognise, pause before you open it. Hold it in your hands and do a mini 'reading' on it. What can you pick up? After a bit of practice, you will probably pick up some image and, if it's from a friend or relative, you may even get a flash of their face briefly in front of you. You can play the same game when you're given a present. Hold it a minute before opening it and see if you can sense anything. You won't necessarily see the object inside clearly in your mind but you may get a 'flash' of something related: if it's a vase, for example, you might see a bunch of pretty flowers, or if it's a scarf, you might see the giver of the gift suddenly entering a clothing store. If you are with a friend or relative, ask them to try an experiment for you. Ask them to put an object, any object, within a sealed container of some sort: a box or envelope. Then hold the sealed object and see what you get from it. You might find doing these experiments under relaxed conditions helps you; if you don't feel under such pressure to produce the right results, chances are the results will be good!

Once you start becoming aware of the aura that objects give out and start tapping in to these different energies, it gives you an even greater appreciation of how fascinating psychic work can be. Imagine what it could be like for an experienced psychic going into an antique shop! All those different objects, all holding a wealth of information and energies. Of course, an experienced medium knows how to shut themselves down tightly in such a situation: suddenly being bombarded by all that information at once would be impossible to handle. Next time you go into an antique shop, see what you sense. Notice how different shops have a very different feeling. Never try to consciously open up to do this – it isn't necessary with so much energy there to begin with – but do always remember to cleanse thoroughly.

There are specially gifted mediums who work with police using psychometry. For intance, if an item of clothing has been found at the scene of a crime, police have been known to contact certain psychics to ask them what they can pick up on the item to help trace the criminal. It can be a wonderfully rewarding aspect of psychic work but it can also be difficult and distressing, requiring a great inner strength on behalf of the medium.

You read earlier that stones and crystals aren't a good choice for beginners. The reason is that their vibrations can be so strong and, on occasions, distressing. There have been instances where a psychic held a piece of lava from a volcano and was seized with an indescribable feeling of terror and suffocation; or they held a rock from a battlefield that left them feeling utterly traumatised and overwhelmed with grief. Protect and nurture yourself by leaving experiences like that until you are a mature psychic.

If you do work well with psychometry, you can develop a finely tuned affinity with objects. There was a series of tests conducted in America in the late 1800's, where a psychic was sent small scraps of blank paper, torn from the letters of various well-known people. There was nothing written on the papers (which were cut from just below each signature) apart from Gentleman No. 1, Lady No. 2 etc. Records from the time show the psychic's readings were remarkably accurate.

There are many other fascinating examples of psychometric experiences. Old records detail an extraordinary event which occurred during 1642 on the Oxfordshire/ Warwickshire borders. The Battle of Edgehill took place on the 23rd October, but two months later a number of shepherds and village people actually 'heard' the battle taking place again: gunfire, horses neighing, moans of the wounded. The phenomenon lasted several hours and because so many people of repute confirmed their experience, King Charles I sent a commission out to the spot to investigate. They also had a similar experience.

Another interesting event occurred during the 1800's on

the Clyde, a few miles below Lanark, when a large group of people 'witnessed' a spectacle in front of them. The ground and trees appeared littered with a shower of hats and guns, men were marching in ranks etc. The odd detail here is that only two thirds of the group present actually saw this happening, and the other third saw and heard nothing.

If you enquire further into psychic phenomena, you will uncover many more examples such as these, often dating back to ancient times. It's a comforting thought to know that what you are dealing with is an increased level of awareness that has, in fact, been around and been experienced for a long time.

Chapter 9:
FLOWER READING

Flower reading is also known as flower clairsentience or flower psychometry and although it's not as widely used as auric reading and other psychometry, it's a very powerful form of 'reading' somebody. Basically, your sitter holds a living flower for a brief while, then hands you the flower to 'read'. You then use the flower's vibrations to tune in to your sitter. This sounds complicated and may seem rather fanciful but do try it out, at least once, as the unerring accuracy may amaze you. It's best if you have worked with auric reading and psychometry before you try this, as the vibrations are slightly different here. Whereas the auric reading and psychometry are generally dealing with the 'here and now' of the person, flower reading goes onto another level, taking you back into someone's early life and also dealing very much with their spiritual nature. You need to have worked with the other two types of readings to understand the difference. For flower reading, you will be using the heart chakra for the first time. The solar plexus and spleen chakras, which you have been using up to now, have been described as the feeling, emotional centres in the body and therefore you have been tapping in to people very much on that level. Now, using the heart chakra, you are starting to work in a slightly different area, becoming aware of subtler vibrations. In the case of flower reading, the heart chakra will help you tap in to the deeper spiritual needs of a person and the feelings you have when working with the flower will be different from auric reading and psychometry.

You can use any type of flower provided it's fresh, not dried or artificial, and provided it has a stem at least three inches long. It should preferably be handled only by your sitter before they hand it over to you. If someone else has to hold it in the process, it should only be handled through another substance, such as paper. The ideal would be for your sitter to pick a flower of choice from their own garden, as different flowers reveal different aspects of a person. A thick-stemmed, heavy flower will show the stronger nature, a soft, wispy flower will tell you about their softer, inner emotions. If your sitter can choose the flower for themselves, it means they are also choosing, albeit subconsciously, which aspect of themselves they can benefit from looking at. Of course, not everyone has a garden and, if not, it's best if they choose a flower themselves from a florist or friend.

Your sitter only needs to hold the flower for a short while before they hand it on to you. Whilst they're holding it, they don't need to concentrate or think of anything in particular. In fact, have a cup of tea or coffee and have a chat or just relax! Let them run their hands up and down the stem and lightly over the flower head – that is all they need to do. This isn't an exercise on thought-transference: the flower's vibrations work on a much subtler, more spiritual level than that. Whilst they are making contact with the flower, you can concentrate on the opening-up process, making sure you feel comfortable and ready to work. Remember that you have to take the energies up to the heart centre now and it may take you a little longer to do that. The more you have practised moving your energies up and down in your psychic lift (as detailed in chapter five), the easier this will be for you now.

When you're both ready, have your sitter hand you the flower. Take it lightly in your hands, close your eyes and start from the base of the stem. This represents your sitter's early life, from birth, and as you work your way up the stem, so you are going through their life up to the present, which is the head of the flower. The head of the flower then reveals most about the spiritual nature of your sitter. It may be their spiritual needs, their aspirations, the path they are meant to tread in life: it can be a variety of aspects that you will pick up on.

So, starting with the base, slowly make your way upwards. Although you don't need to rush this process, don't stop and dwell on a particular aspect for a long time. The smoother your journey up the flower, the easier it will be for you to keep a flow of contact and conversation. For this reason, it will help if your sitter doesn't speak until you have finished the reading, so ask if they can keep all their comments until the end. Every time you speak, remember to then renew your energies up to your heart again. You may keep lifting only to your spleen to begin with, as this is all you have known until now. If that happens, let the energy drop again straight away and then take another breath and lift up as far as the heart. It will take you a while to master this next level.

Speak as soon as you sense something. You may see flashes of your sitter as a baby, or see objects which meant something to them in their childhood or feel overwhelming emotions relating to their childhood. Even as you feel the sensations, keep moving slowly up the stem. You will probably find messages coming to you more quickly in this process. The reason is that your sitter's energies are moving onto a faster dimension as the flower's vibrations are actually speeding them up. This is why it can be a powerful and accurate form of psychometry.

As you work your way up the flower, try to give a rough idea of age as you comment on parts of their life, as otherwise your sitter may be confused. However, you don't need to open your eyes and see how far up the stem you are to calculate the years. You may see them in your mind and know their age that way or see the number in front of your eyes, or else you may just 'know' they were approximately that age. You may also have sections of their life which won't yield any information for you, perhaps because your sitter chooses not to look at that part of their life at that time. Don't dwell on anything unpleasant or upsetting. After all, most of us have had rough patches in our life which have left sadnesses in us but it doesn't usually help us to have them dragged up again. If you instinctively feel it is beneficial to pass comment such as 'You went through a difficult patch in your late 20's but you have learnt from it and become stronger as a result' – that is fine. Negative comments should always have a positive added to them. Cleanse constantly if you pick up uncomfortable feelings and then lift your energies up to the heart again.

As you reach the head of the flower, you will probably have stronger emotional and spiritual reactions. Sometimes as you touch the head of the flower, it can be like an explosion of feeling or understanding. On this level, using your heart as well as solar plexus and spleen, you will be able to give a deeper reading. Until you experience this for yourself, it's hard to describe it. You will say something because you 'know' it; not because someone has told you, or because you see it clearly in your head, but because you 'know'. You're working on a different vibration and once you experience it, you will always be able to tell the difference. As you linger over the head of the flower, you may find yourself saying things you never expected to say, on a level of understanding you hadn't consciously thought about before. You may see more symbols than usual, but this time you will be able to clarify their meaning, whereas before you weren't certain. You can see deeper into the core of someone's spirituality on this level and you may even be able to 'see' where they want to go, or need to go next on their spiritual path. You may be able to tell if they are blocking themselves or trying to push themselves too hard. At this stage, you will probably know yourself when the reading is over, as you will feel your energies suddenly drop of their own accord. Always try to finish a reading, especially one on this deeper level, with something positive and encouraging to your sitter.

Take a moment to cleanse yourself and renew your energies before you open your eyes again. Focus on an object to ground yourself or use the image of your feet with roots attached to them, growing deep into the ground. You've been working on a higher vibration and it may take you an extra minute to come back down to earth and be able to focus properly on your sitter.

Now you've finished, ask them for feed-back. It's best to start with the bits they couldn't understand. Check to make sure it wasn't your phraseology that was confusing and/or your incorrect interpretation of something. Even at this stage, it will be hard for you not to let your own brain interfere on certain levels. Another example: you saw a large glass filled with yellow liquid during their late teenage years and assume they were a great beer drinker. They were teetotal, but they were addicted to apple juice!

There will always be some inaccuracies when you are a beginner and also the 'opposites' will crop up, such as you interpreting a dislike of something as being a love, but chances are you will find the medium of flower reading to be one of the most accurate.

A few people find it a completely uninspiring form of psychometry and if you're one of those, don't worry about it, but do try flower reading with more than one person and preferably with different types of flowers before giving up on it. If you remain untouched by it, you will no doubt find your talents lie in other directions in these chapters.

Chapter 10:
HEALING

There are many levels of healing: from the simplest touch of a loved one's hand on our brow soothing our pain, to the highly intricate, skilled diagnostic treatment of a trained psychic such as Dr. Edgar Cayce. This book will only deal with healing on the psychic, emotional level but there is a great deal you can do in this sphere to safely help others.

Most of us have received unconscious healing at times in our lives. As a child, did a parent gently rub your stomach when you felt unwell, or stroke your forehead when you had a headache, so that you felt soothed, calmed? Or when you've felt hurt or upset, has your cat or dog come and sat next to you and made you feel better? Or have you come home at the end of a rough day at work and had a loved one put their arms around you, which has eased the troubles you were feeling? All these are examples of healing which have been taking place in various forms ever since man began. The Scriptures make many references to the 'laying on of hands' but it has also been continually been mentioned throughout history.

There is even an interesting connection with British Royalty and the healing process. Since the time of Edward III, the kings of England were deemed to have a healing touch. Edward III actually bathed the sufferer's afflicted areas, although this was gradually phased out by further monarchs who made do with a touch from the royal hand. This practice continued at least up until 1745. Thereafter, coins which had been touched by the royal hand were deemed to offer a similar power. They were called 'royal touch pieces' and several exist still today in British museums. However, there's no need for you to be royalty or hold a coin to offer your healing powers to someone! The method can be much simpler than that.

Is there someone you know who is unwell? You can send them healing thoughts without them even being in the room, or without them even knowing about it. This is called absent healing and it's been shown to be extremely effective.

To do this, you need to be in your comfortable space, with no phones, children or animals to burst in on you, affording relative peace and quiet. To start with, choose just one person who you know needs some healing. You can increase the number after a little practice but one person will make your visualisation easier.

Go through your usual breathing and opening-up process, really concentrating on the energy of the white light in the room and lifting the energies as high as the heart level. When you feel opened up and ready to work, create a mental picture of the person you want to heal in the centre of the room. Regardless of their condition at present, see them as happy, well and joyous. This is extremely important. Visualising someone as a whole, functioning soul is part of the healing process. There's no benefit in seeing someone as depressed or ill in any way. Forget how they looked or sounded when you last saw them or spoke to them. If they were in pain or sadness, imagine them free of all pain and smiling. Picture them in the very pink of health, joyous on the outside and the inside. Then imagine the beautiful, pure white light shining down upon them, filling them with energy, health and joy. Bathe them in the healing light and feel them enjoy the benefits of it. Surround their body with your love as well as the universal love. Then send the image of that person, well and healthy, up to the Great Universal Spirit above. To some that may be God or Allah or Buddha – it doesn't matter what religious or spiritual belief you hold, as that is up to you. You can then repeat this process as often as you like for others. Cleansing is particularly important after this work. You may not realise but you might have temporarily picked up some of their symptoms. In other words, by imagining them as well and happy, you may have unconsciously taken some of their unwell vibrations or sadnesses into your own aura. A trained psychic would never do this but in your learning stages it is possible to do so. Let everything you have picked up disperse, so you also feel refreshed again afterwards.

It isn't necessary for you to tell the person that you are about to do some absent healing on them. The wonder of the process is that it can work even without the receiver knowing what is happening. Or, if you prefer, tell them you will send out your healing at a certain hour of the day and then confer later to see if they felt any change. On the level at which you are working, you may find the effect is slight because you can often be dealing with someone on a subtle, unconscious level.

You can also do a mini-healing should a friend or relative phone and mention that they have, for example, a headache. Simply imagine their head cradled in your arms as you speak to them and gently stroke their head. Again, remember to cleanse after the conversation.

Some people like to use colours to help their concentration. However, colours are very powerful and if the colour you visualise is inappropriate for their condition, it may hinder rather than help them. As a general rule, green, the colour of love and the heart chakra, is the safest to use. So if you really feel you need to add colour to help the process, send out a warm, grass-green colour. Rose pink is also a very calming, soothing colour if someone is agitated and highly strung – but not suitable if the person is feeling chronically worn-out, as it won't rejuvenate them. When in doubt, use the pure white light to surround them, healing and energising.

Plants have been known to respond wonderfully well to healing techniques. If you have a plant that is looking straggly or generally sorry for itself, try talking to it, or stroking the leaves gently, or simply sending out your healing energy to the plant's aura. You may choose to be alone in the room when you do this! Of course it can feel odd when you first do it, but it's not as crazy as it sounds. The truth is that a great deal of research has been done over the years to support the theory that plants react to whatever is around them. This attitude goes back a long way in history. In Hindu mythology, it is said that enchanting flute music from Shri Krishna made flowers bloom. Tamil literature describes how sugarcanes grow in response to the musical sounds of beetles, wasps and bees.

There are also many well-documented examples of animals responding to the healing touch. Possibly the reason they react so favourably is because they are not preprogrammed as we humans are with such cynicism and doubt. They respond instinctively, not intellectually. As you'll be discovering for yourself, our human mind can get in the way a great deal with psychic work.

You can also try 'hands-on' healing with someone present. You need to be clear with your sitter that the form of healing you can offer is not some sort of all-effective cure and you can guarantee no results. Whatever medication or treatment they may already be receiving should not be altered in any way or influenced by you. As a beginner, you can offer comfort and, possibly, an ability to relax them and release some pain. You cannot offer any sort of diagnosis on this level, or cure for anything they may have. Often people who seek healing are in a very low frame of mind and it's important you don't offer them false hopes.

As far as your sitter is concerned, it is not necessary for them to have 'faith' to be helped. (That is why absent healing can be powerful). They don't have to have faith in you or your methods of healing. What they do need to believe in, however, is their own ability to change. In other words, nothing in them is immovable and irreparable. That attitude towards the possibility of change is extremely important. Someone who feels nobody and nothing can ever affect them will be so resistant to any assistance that they will probably block all penetration of their aura. Talk to your sitter before you offer healing and try to gain an understanding of them before you start. (It is rather as if you are tuning in to their aura as you speak.)

It's also important that you have great respect and sensitivity during a healing session. Remember that their aura is actually part of them (even if they don't realise it) and by going into their aura and working with their energies, you are, in effect, touching them, sometimes on quite a deep spiritual level. It may help if you have a few quiet words with your own god or guide and actually ask for permission to heal the person. Most people aren't very in touch with their spiritual side so they can find this a bit of a shock and quite intrusive. It's up to you, by your manner, to be as calming and reassuring as possible. They won't be able to relax unless you help them.

It's up to you and your sitter together to decide which position they choose during the healing session. Most people will initially choose to sit upright. Standing feels awkward and lying down may seem too vulnerable at first. Once you have gained their confidence, and increased your own in the process, you may find that for them to lie down makes it easier for you to administer healing on certain parts of them. They may also end up feeling more relaxed that way but it may take a few sittings before you reach that level.

It's particularly appropriate during healing work to offer a quiet prayer beforehand and afterwards. As already stated earlier in this book, this need not be religious in any way, although if you have a strong religious faith that guides you, use that, or whatever is meaningful for you. You need not speak your prayer out loud as it may not make your sitter comfortable. Try asking them before you begin whether they would like you to say a few words or not. If they prefer nothing, it's still fine for you to offer your own silent prayer.

There is no need for you to physically touch your sitter during healing work. Many people aren't comfortable with physical communication and it can be misconstrued under sensitive conditions. You are purely using energies within auras to comfort and cleanse and if you want to maintain a professional approach with your sitter, it's easier to do so working with their aura and not their physical body. It's just as effective to work this way.

It's especially important that you open up properly for healing sessions. Unless there is a flow of energy running smoothly through your body, you won't be an effective instrument in your work. You will also be vulnerable to taking in upsets or illnesses from their aura and holding these within your own. So remember to keep that flow of white light going through your body during the healing process. You will also need the energy to be free-flowing through your arms and hands, so pay particular attention to these areas. Make sure you feel completely open before you start and well cleansed.

Healing on the level you are working with, goes up as far as the heart chakra, so you need to bring your psychic lift up to that level. If you have been practising flower reading, you will be better used to this level. If not, it may take you some time and a few sittings before you feel right about healing work.

You can ask your sitter if they have a particular area on which they'd like you to concentrate, such as a headache, or neck or backache. If they don't want to specify any area, use your own tuning in to feel which part of them would most benefit from healing. You may find, although your sitter asks you to deal with one part of their body, that you feel drawn to treat another area as well.

Avoid spending much time either at the crown of the head or around the heart chakra (front and back for the latter).

These are very sensitive areas: the crown because it is always open and receiving energy and the heart because it deals with the person's respiratory system, a 'core' of their being. A more experienced healer may spend some considerable time in these areas and be safe to do so but you should be very careful in your early stages. Pass over the crown and heart areas but do not linger long around them.

As you move your hands around and through your sitter's aura, remember to keep cleansing and renewing your energies. Bring the energy up to your heart chakra each time you breathe in. Once you have done a few healing sessions and gained some experience and confidence in your ability, you will soon find your hands drawn to certain areas, usually without knowing quite why.

When you find an area on which you want to stay for a while, then you can use your energy in a different way. You need to imagine the pure, white energy coming into you, passing down your arms and hands and pouring out through your fingers. Doing this allows healing vibrations to act through you (rather than from you), passing from your aura and into your sitter's. Again, this is why you need to keep the energy flowing. It shouldn't be your own energy that is passing out of your hands and fingers; you should only be the instrument through which the pure, cosmic energy is flowing. Ideally, what is happening is that the pure white energy is being further energised by your loving, healing thoughts and the two together complement each other, providing a powerful means of helping others. As a beginner, it is easy to get carried away with what is a very giving, loving sensation and to thus use your own energy a great deal. You will soon know if you are doing this because you will feel drained, washed out and even slightly depressed afterwards. If this happens, you should stop offering healing to others until you have re-energised yourself and you should then practise in small doses on other people. After healing someone, you should be left with a clean, refreshed feeling and the sensation of being uplifted. Always cleanse thoroughly before you close down at the end and offer a small prayer of thanks in your own way.

You will soon find different sitters have very different reactions to what you do. Some will feel literally nothing but it doesn't mean something hasn't shifted on a subtle level somewhere, of which they aren't yet aware. Others may have very strong sensations of something happening or moving or shifting but they won't actually know what or be able to clearly explain the sensation. Some will feel very clear temperatures of either hot or cold, dependent upon the healer's vibrations, rather like hot air or a cool fan blowing onto them. Some sitters talk of feeling a heavy cloud lifting off their shoulders or some other part of their anatomy, others a wonderfully calming sense of well-being and alignment. Some feel pain easing out of sore or stressed muscles.

Occasionally, your sitter may experience discomfort in some area. If that happens, cleanse them with the pure, white light above them. Visualise it going through their body and washing away any pain. You may choose to do this, anyway, as part of the healing process.

Your reactions will also vary according to your own method of working. Some healers feel very little themselves. They work on an intuitive level, knowing instinctively to go to a certain area and concentrate on healing, because they 'know' it to be right. Or you may tune in to somebody aurically as you are healing, in which case you may briefly feel their symptoms or stresses for a moment before you heal them. Again, you must cleanse those feelings from you as you work. This does mean you can find yourself cleansing literally dozens of times through one healing session. Other healers get incredibly strong tingling or tickling sensations in their fingers as they work. Their hands may suddenly feel very hot or very cold or very twitchy and itchy. You may have another sensation entirely but after several healing sittings you will soon learn to recognise what happens with you and it will become part of your own process of healing.

If, at any time during a healing session, either you or your sitter suddenly feel very unwell or in pain, you should stop the healing process immediately and spend several minutes cleansing under your waterfall and the white light. Remember that you must be in control of the sitting and you have the ability to remove unwanted influences. You must exercise that right to get rid of unpleasant effects as soon as they crop up. It's important that your sitter has complete confidence in you and can relax, knowing you are in full control of what you are doing.

Some healers choose to use crystals while they are working. They either hold them in their hands while they work or have them present somewhere in the room. It's well known that crystals have powerful energies but they are still, nevertheless, only a tool to increase effectiveness.

Quartz crystals are a natural substance, made from movements in the earth's crust. The molecular structure of the quartz crystal affords it a perfect alignment and symmetry and it therefore has very special physical properties. It can receive, amplify, convert and focus energy – even store an electrical charge. That is why people believe crystals have the ability to focus and modify the pure, cosmic energy we use in psychic work. A crystal in a room is said to bring harmony and peace. One placed in drinking water is said to give the water a better flavour and neutralise its impurities. Some people keep one in their refrigerator, as they believe it keeps food fresh and pure. Others place crystals around the bath, which they then believe turns the bathing process into a cleansing, revitalising spiritual experience. Likewise, many healers use crystals to reduce pain and amplify the healing procedure.

Choosing the right crystal is not easy and shouldn't be rushed. You're best advised to spend some time looking in different shops and to really tune in to the crystal and its energy before you purchase it. If you decide to do so, then the crystal must be 'cleansed' before you use it. Either place it in a clear, running stream if you have one near you or soak it in salt water. Some people actually 'charge' the crystal by using their own breath and breathing over it for a period of time. As a beginner, you may not want to use this extra tool yet, but you could consider it for the future if healing becomes a powerful expression of psychic work for you.

Chapter 11:
PSYCHIC DRAWING

There are some psychics who work best by using pens or pencils and drawing. Images come out through their hand rather than in their mind. You may already have heard of very famous psychic artists who actually draw portraits of people who have passed over onto the other side of life. They had to spend a great deal of their life working to attain this ability and it's not suggested that you can progress to a level such as that, but you may find drawing is a way of developing your psychic potential. You won't know unless you try it, although it's said that budding psychic artists often experience twinges or a tickling sensation in their fingers or hand when they start tuning in. Some also find their hands go very hot or very cold. Whether or not you have had any experiences like that so far, do try the following one day.

Sit opposite your sitter and go through the usual opening-up and tuning-in process, taking your energy up to your solar plexus, but this time have a large, hard-backed pad on your lap and a pen or pencil (a pencil is usually easier to start with). Hold the pencil loosely in your hand with the tip just resting on the open pad. You don't have to keep your eyes closed but it may help your concentration if you do. Don't consciously move your hand at all, but let the energy be freeflowing through you. In other words, feel the energy coming through your body and down your arm and into your hand and fingers (as with the healing work). You don't need to picture an image and then draw it with your eyes closed because this isn't an exercise to test your artistic skill. This is about opening up psychically without using your conscious mind. Try to let the pencil start working under its own steam without you deliberately forcing any activity –

just as you tried to keep your own thoughts out of it when you verbally reported images and feelings. You don't even need to be aware of what it is you are drawing. Let your hand feel free and unrestrained and don't question your movements at all. Keep drawing until your hand stops of its own accord but do try to keep the energy circling around throughout. Once you're sure the drawing is finished, then open your eyes and look at it.

One of two things will then probably happen: 1) You quite quickly see a shape, symbol or message within the drawing which you can interpret or, 2) You burst into laughter at the indecipherable mess you have created! If it's the latter, possibly this form of psychic drawing isn't for you but you should try on another occasion or two before being certain. If it's the former, then this may turn into a useful medium for you. Perhaps you can tune in better and clear your own thoughts when you're drawing. You may find you draw clear pictures and symbols which you instantly recognise or the drawing may be more abstract, requiring interpretation. Give your own 'reading' before showing it to your sitter and asking if they want to comment further.

Another area of psychic drawing that can be very revealing is to try doing an 'auragraph'. This is exactly what it sounds like: a graph of someone's aura. The word 'graph' is misleading because it implies a mathematically neat arrangement, but auragraphs can be as irregular and freeflowing as you wish. You need coloured crayons or pastels for this and preferably eight different colours: the seven rainbow or chakra colours plus a white. (You can start off with more colours if you wish but it will make your interpretation of the drawing more difficult at this stage.) You also need a sheet of large, plain paper, such as an A3-size.

Sit down with your sitter (or stand if you have an easel against which you can work) and tune in as you would for an auric reading. Remember how you have to keep that spiral of energy going, with your aura reaching out via your solar plexus towards their solar plexus, and then drawing their aura back into yours and bringing it close to you. Get this perpetual circle of energy flowing well before you try to start. When you feel well tuned-in and relaxed, decide which colour you want to pick up first and then, without thinking or analysing too much, let your pastel or crayon sweep across the paper in whatever design or shape feels right for your sitter. Draw with it until you feel the energy drop again in you, and then pick up another colour. You may find some people make you want to use every colour you have and more – others may seem only suited to one or two colours. Always try to tune in before picking up a colour and don't rush the process. As soon as you stop your regular breathing, that energy and information will drop again, so keep spiralling. When you feel you have done enough for your sitter, stop, step back and study what you have drawn.

Remember, although it's called an auragraph, you don't have to draw neat colours emanating from a human shape. This exercise is to free you from conscious thought, so your final result can be whatever shape and colour you want it to be. You might initially feel at a loss to understand the meaning of your drawing, or you may have already been aware what each colour you used was referring to in your sitter's life.

The reason it's suggested that you start off with only the seven chakra colours is because you can tune in and read the drawing based on your understanding of those colours. Here is a run-down of what the colours relate to in order to help you interpret what you draw:

Red: the physical, earth part of us, including our primal instinct for survival. Deals with the material aspect of life. Also physical energy, passion and feelings of anger. Sometimes red can be appropriate when dealing with childhood because it's also considered to represent the 'root' of a person.

Orange: our relationships with others, our ability to share and be intimate. Also deals with sexual feelings. Very much a feeling, emotional colour and often relates to ambition.

Yellow: our sense of self, our purpose, destiny and willpower. Also an intellectual colour, related to thinking and working hard.

Green: loving and giving but not just in relationships, as it also relates to a larger, universal love that is unconditional and limitless. Also a healing and nurturing colour.

Blue: speech, communication, creativity and self-expression. Relates also to lisening to your own 'inner voice' and meditation. Also shows sensitivity. A calm and expansive colour, like the limitless expanse of the sky.

Purple: the mind and spiritual intellect. Relates to intuition and far-seeing knowledge, also dreams and memories. Represents a move towards spiritual connection and understanding. This colour is about transcending physical, material levels.

Violet or White: purity and the highest degree of spiritual awareness. Relates to self-realisation, fulfilment and enlightenment. Also represents completion.

The shapes you use are also significant and part of your analysis. Wavy lines shows movement, fluidity, but also a fluctuating state within your sitter. Straight lines show clear purpose. Solid blocks of colour can mean determination, great influences or large blocks in their life. Circles can show cycles or life patterns. You may be drawn to actual symbols which mean certain things to you: the sun for a bright disposition, the moon for a mystical quality, the star for a star personality etc. Areas or lines that start off as definite and then wisp away into nothingness usually show a part of life that has been allowed to escape, or that your sitter chose to eradicate from their life.

Here are a few examples to start you thinking and interpreting auragraphs:

• You've drawn two wavy lines across the page using just yellow and purple, as no other colours felt appropriate. How can you read such a basic drawing? Ask yourself what yellow and purple mean to you, using the above run-down as a guide. Purple could mean their spirituality and yellow their determination and thought processes into trying to deal with that aspect of their life. The waviness of it would tend to indicate that your sitter is moving along this path but unsure about certain aspects of it: either their goals, their abilities or their own strengths. You can then tune in to the drawing to try and gain a deeper understanding and to give a richer reading. What appears at first to be simple and uninspiring will often turn out to be much more meaningful than you ever could have believed.

• You've drawn a solid line of blue across the bottom of the page and on it rests a large green box, out of which green streamers are flowing. What does the solid line of blue say to you? Perhaps there's a great calm at the base of this person, someone who is good at meditation and contemplation. The green box with streamers would indicate a very giving, loving person, someone who feels secure with their own sense of selfworth, whilst not afraid to give and share. The more streamers you have drawn, the better they are at giving. But notice if the green box is full of colour or empty. If there is only the outline of the box, that would tend to show that this person gives out a great deal without necessarily checking their own reserves first. A solid green box would show someone very capable of keeping themselves full of love and light. The absence of any purple or yellow might indicate that they are not great intellectuals and that spiritual awareness is not a great attraction. A lack of red or orange may show a disinterest in the physical side of life. That is not a criticism, and in no way detracts from their capacity for love, merely an observation to increase your understanding of a drawing.

• You've drawn big, inter-connecting swirls of red and orange that fill the page and then, up in the corner, but not touching in any way, are small blobs of green and purple. You know the picture is certainly bold and expressive but what does it express? Red and orange are very physical, earth colours, so this would tend to show that your sitter is very physically-oriented, and possibly sex is very important to them. They are passionate about life, but not necessarily on a mental or spiritual level. The fact that you chose large swirls shows they express themselves well in this aspect of their life but there seems to be no real sense of purpose or intended outcome. They also probably don't think a great deal before getting involved in relationships, work-wise or personally, as they deal mainly on the physical level, not concentrating on emotional and mental aspects. However, you also drew blobs of green and purple. That would indicate that they are aware there is another part of life that they haven't yet tapped into, but they know it is there, possibly on a subconscious level. As it's not literally connected to them, it may take them a while before they consider that aspect of their lives but by virtue of the green and purple being there, it seems likely that, at some point, they will want to discover more about the loving and spiritual side of their nature. Again, this is not to detract from them as a person now, or to imply there is a part of their life that they are missing. There is nothing wrong with someone enjoying life entirely on the physical level. Everyone has their own karmic route to follow and it's not for you to judge or advise, but to read what you see without trying to influence.

These are fairly basic examples that you shouldn't have too much trouble analysing and it's likely that when you first start drawing auragraphs, you will also draw relatively uncomplicated pictures. With time, they may become more complex and require a deeper interpretation, provided this becomes a useful tool for you. You will then find that you develop your own way of working – and it's quite possible that for you the colours may come to have different meanings. There is nothing wrong with that as long as you explain to your sitter what the colour represents to you so that they can understand the drawing and not misinterpret it. In other words, feel free to develop your own style but, as you do so, make sure you are clearly communicating your drawings' meanings.

If you do want to continue with auragraph work, it would help you to develop a greater understanding of colour and how it affects everyone. There are a lot of good books on the subject that cover all aspects of colour in considerable depth. Studying some of these is necessary to enhance your capacity for work and interpretation.

Chapter 12:
BLOCKS AND DIFFICULTIES: HOW TO DEAL WITH THEM

Once you have experimented with the previous chapters in this book, you will have discovered more about yourself. You will have found out that you are better in some work than others. Someone who is very effective giving auric readings may not work so well with psychometry. Some of you may have discovered you have an affinity for healing techniques but find that flower reading leaves you utterly cold. You will all be developing your own methods of opening and closing the chakras and creating the colours and you'll be starting to develop your own style with your readings. If you see mainly symbols, you'll have started interpreting them, and you'll have created a greater ability for leaving your own mind and thoughts out of your psychic work in general. You should acknowledge the improvements you have made in your development and take heart from them.

You will also have started to get 'blocks' and be confused by them. Working with so many energies is a confusing business (remember the concept that we have over 72,000 nadis running through our bodies?!) and as you progress, various hiccups will crop up that you'll find frustrating. In fact, they are all part of your growth and necessary for you in your learning process.

Some days you'll feel as though you are literally flying: your readings will have a high degree of accuracy and people will feel the benefit of what you have offered. Other days will find you grumpy and insecure about your abilities: you'll receive little or no information and what you do get through won't be readily understood by your sitters. There are a variety of reasons for these blocks, so below are a few possibilities for you to consider.

Firstly, look at the room in which you were working. Was it too cold? Or too hot? Were there strong-smelling flowers creating an atmosphere or were there distracting odours such as new paint or an over-powering room freshener?

As a beginner, the more you can practise your work in a room which feels right for you, the more it will aid you: a space you can call your own without constant outside influences. If you have the means to paint it the colour you want and furnish it the way you want, go ahead and do so. (Remember to avoid very dark colours, as they absorb light and energy). Some people don't feel a room is alive until it has living houseplants in it; others only feel comfortable with dried or artificial flowers. Bare floorboards mean comfort to one person and barren coldness to another. Some find lighting a candle increases the vibrations in the room. Some like gentle music in the background; others need complete silence. As this is, hopefully, your own small space, make sure it is right for you.

Then look at yourself. Although we are drawing in outside energy to work, if you are very tired, as a beginner that will certainly affect you. Did you get enough sleep the night before?

Were you extremely hungry and unable to concentrate properly? Or were you feeling very bloated after a large meal and found it impossible to forget your heavy stomach? It's always best to eat light meals before you practise psychic work, preferably a couple of hours before you work.

Alcohol and psychic work don't mix either. Even a glass of wine can have an effect on your own energies and those around you. By all means have a drink afterwards, to celebrate a successful reading, but have one before and chances are there won't be anything to celebrate! Needless to say, any form of drugs comes under the same category.

Once you started working, had you properly left your own troubles and stresses behind? In other words, had you really cleansed yourself of your own problems before you started? It is hard to let go of persistent worries but it's a great discipline to learn for all your life, not just for psychic work, and if you can teach yourself to let go of all of 'you' when you open up, your results will be much more effective. You have to remember that we are only using our body and mind as an instrument to receive outside messages and the best instrument is a clean, well-oiled one.

As you go through your opening-up process, you may suddenly find one chakra is more difficult to open than another, either because you just can't seem to visualise the colour properly or because it simply won't open for you. There can be a variety of reasons for this, all personal. Have you just been deeply hurt by someone you love and trust? The solar plexus or heart may be a little less willing to open up. Are you longing to tell your boss what you really think of his new employee regulations? Your throat may be feeling restricted. Are you feeling extremely angry over something that has recently occurred? Your spleen might be affected. Do you have a stomach ache? Your solar plexus may not feel like opening up. Of course, the ideal is to be able to cleanse those conditions away whilst you work, so go back to your pure white light and the waterfall and again cleanse through before trying to open further. Even on good days, you'll find it's naturally easier to open some chakras than others, just as some colours may be easier for you to visualise than others. Continual practice will enable you to improve but when you hit a block on a particular energy centre, remember to be kind to yourself. The more you push to try to clear the block, the more you will hinder yourself. Take a quiet moment to tune in to yourself to see what feels wrong, then cleanse again.

Another block may come up if you are working with someobody else, or you are reading various books on psychic work and it suddenly seems as if nobody is working quite the way you work and it makes you feel uncomfortable and insecure. Our natural instinct is to want to follow the herd and if we find ourselves being pointed in a different direction, it can be very disconcerting. We then clam up in confusion. You need to know that every psychic works in specific ways and however you are developing is right for you. Just because your friend opens up very quickly and you take five minutes, doesn't matter. The fact that you may only sense things and somebody else sees all these vivid, colourful images, doesn't make either one of you better than the other. Your friend may pick up a pencil and be able to draw wonderful pictures which are full of rich meaning while you sit there with a motionless pencil for ten minutes! Don't compare or try to compete with others and be proud to be individual in your growth. No two auras are alike, so why should people themselves try to be alike? Embracing your own unique talents will clear other blocks in you.

Another common problem is that you rarely progress at an even rate in psychic work. You may stay at the same level for a long time, and then move forward rapidly, only to suddenly stop again and not progress further for ages. It can be very frustrating: the irritating sense of not moving forward, followed by the pleasure when you do, followed by the irritating brake system all over again! This is a natural development process, as you can only move forward to another level when you are ready. The frustration comes when you are certain you are ready yourself but still nothing shifts. The reason is because those higher and wiser than you know you aren't ready yet to deal with another level. Again, the more you push against this, the longer it will take you to move on. Accept each level you are on, and know you will move forward when you are ready to do so. Accept the 'fits and starts' system as normal in this work.

If you have an unsuccessful sitting (and everyone has one occasionally, even experienced psychics) look to the points mentioned above and if none of those seems to fit the occasion, then, and only then, think about your sitter. Did they want to be there in the first place or did they have to be coerced into being your sitter? Were they very closed to the whole psychic experience and not interested in what you had to say anyway? Did they say 'no' to everything, almost before you had finished a sentence? Or were they extremely nervous and worried about the whole experience and not able to relax at all? Were they so nervous that they retracted their aura close to them, making your work very difficult? There will always be people who are very cynical about psychic work, as well as those who are frightened of it, and any of those emotions make it hard for you to work successfully. See it as a real 'test' for yourself and do your best to alleviate their fear and insecurities by explaining the basics of psychic work so that you eliminate the 'voodoo' element of it. Try using a very simple analogy to explain something such as auric reading to them. For instance, you could say 'Your aura is just like a homemade video of your life and all I'm doing in reading your aura is borrowing your video and running it through my projector which is my mind'. They may not completely understand you, but it may somewhat reassure them. Once you have done a few sittings, you will be able to work out for yourself what is going on with each sitter and how best to handle each person.

The more you develop your psychic gifts, the more you may notice changes in yourself, not always for the better. As you become more and more sensitive to energies around you, you may find yourself less on an even keel, emotionally and physically. That's why you must be gentle with yourself, especially initially. You are truly developing an appreciation of human and universal energies, how they work and how powerful they are. It's wonderful to discover, but it has its own drawbacks. Apart from struggling with your own discipline and energies, you are being bombarded by others as well! This can result in you feeling more emotional than usual, and you may feel disoriented and just generally out of sorts at times. Places you once frequented may start to feel uncomfortable. As your awareness increases on a psychic level, so your hearing becomes more attuned. Loud music and raucous voices may disturb you when once you could ignore them. It may take less alcohol for you to feel inebriated. If, for example, you work in a hospital or environment with people who are not always in good health, either emotionally or physically, this may start to affect you more than usual.

If this happens, you need to keep closing down all through the day to keep those emotions in check. The solar plexus, in particular, is a strong centre which we tend to open without realising. Use your psychic cloak of protection whenever you need it. You have the comfort of knowing that no one else knows what you are thinking or doing, so you can repeat the process as much as you like.

If at any time you feel you are being attacked by unpleasant energies or emotions, there are additional measures you can take to protect yourself. Hopefully, many of you will never need to use these methods, as you will be going around so well closed down and wrapped up that nothing unwanted can creep through. In case you are feeling vulnerable one day and surrounded by difficult influences, here are some extra steps you can take to deal with it.

You may be with somebody who is showing aggressive or threatening behaviour towards you. Perhaps normally you would laugh it off or otherwise deflect the situation but today you feel under the weather. Instead of reacting angrily yourself, hold an imaginary mirror up to this person, so that their anger is directed back at themselves. You don't need to literally lift your arms and mime a mirror – your thought process alone is powerful enough for them to have a subconscious reaction. Their anger may either stop or fizzle out, or they may just take a step backwards, but they won't know that you have done anything to prompt their sudden cessation in feeling.

Another very powerful way of dealing with someone who is giving you a hard time, is to send out beams of love and light from your heart and solar plexus. Just as you have learnt to reach out with your aura to tap in to someone else's, so you can send out streams of love to calm someone else's upset emotions. It takes strength on your part to do it when all you may feel like returning is a dose of your own anger, but once you feel the benefits of doing it, it becomes easier to repeat. If colour helps you to visualise the process, use streams of green light going from your aura towards the other person.

If you are generally in a situation where you feel uncomfortable and want a quick means of protecting yourself, apart from your own personal psychic cloak, you could simply fold your arms across your solar plexus (a very vulnerable chakra) and cross your ankles. It immediately closes you off from people in a physical way.

There are further visualisation techniques with which you can experiment. You want to feel invisible? Imagine jumping into a brand-new, gleaming dustbin and shutting the lid on top of you. (Always imagine the bin clean and shiny so you don't pick up unhealthy energies. If you find this a claustrophobic image, choose another one). Placing yourself within a clear crystal can also be helpful. Create a beautiful and strong crystal and put yourself into the centre. You can still see out but people can't actually touch you. If that image still seems too restricting, create an imaginary filter screen all around you which allows you to breathe freely and participate in everything around you, but which filters out unhappy and unpleasant vibrations.

If you are in a situation which is making you feel depressed or low in energy, another simple way to protect yourself is to think of something that makes you feel immediately happy: it could be a living being such as your child or pet, or even an object which makes you feel good, or a beautiful setting such as a sunset or rainbow or seascape. Music can also be a great healer of troubled emotions.

If you feel that a room has uncomfortable vibrations in it then you can try lighting some candles, or using a 'smudge stick' (a cleansing candle available from health and new age shops), or burn an aromatherapy oil to cleanse and freshen the room. Eucalyptus, juniper, pine and peppermint are all very good for clearing negative energies from an environment. Or try marjoram, which is an excellent oil for calming if you feel you have taken too much on board, psychically, and want to reduce your sensitivity. It calms a turbulent mind and its emotions.

You may be somebody who responds well to stones and crystals, which are often used as a form of psychic defence. As you've already read, crystals are known to have powerful energies and are often used in psychic work. Listing all the stones and their different healing properties would be a book in itself but here are just a few: amber is particularly good for purifying and drawing out negative energies, jet is helpful for shielding you from negative thoughts, and tiger's eye is renowned for its spiritual protection. Many others are also equally effective.

One last thought for this chapter, and it relates to us all in our daily lives, not just those of you working with psychic development. Everyone is under increasing pressure nowadays, at work and at home, to be the most efficient, the fastest, the very best, at everything we try to do. So often, we all forget just to stop and relax. Even if you can only find five minutes a day, try to be firm about giving yourself that time every day, to sit down, concentrate on your breathing and use your waterfall and light to cleanse and refresh you.

Chapter 13:
PSYCHIC USES IN YOUR DAY-TO-DAY LIFE

You've been reading about how to develop your psychic abilities on various levels, almost all of them involving other people and how to help them. There are also ways in which you can use your psychic work on a day-to-day level to improve conditions for those around you, as well as yourself. This chapter lists just a few small examples of what you can try but no doubt you will start to develop others as you progress.

Have you recently moved and not yet felt as though your new property is quite 'yours'? Or have you in fact been living somewhere for a while and still not felt completely at home no matter what you do? Try this with one of the rooms and see if it makes a difference. Find a few quiet minutes on your own to go and sit in the middle of the room. Try to sit in a comfortable seat and close your eyes. Concentrate on your breathing and relax as much as possible. You can consciously open up if you like but, if you haven't time, you can still do the exercise effectively. Become aware of your aura and expand it a little, using the method detailed in chapter five. Then send out rays of yourself to all corners of the room. It might help if you think of your aura as having long tentacles with which you reach out and brush the walls and floor. Send out loving, healing vibrations as you do so, blessing the room and everything in it. If you wish, say or think a prayer as you send out your vibrations, filling the room with your aura and love. Remember to cleanse, retract your aura, and close down as you finish. Then leave the room for a while and notice when you return if the atmosphere has changed. Some rooms may be easier to imbue with your aura than others, usually depending on the people frequenting the space before you.

Are you leaving your property unattended while you go on holiday and worried about a possible burglary while you're away? (Most of us are!) Apart from taking the usual physical precautions of locked doors and windows, security lights and alarms etc., there is a powerful psychic security system you can use. As you leave your property behind, psychically seal it with protection. You can do this is several ways. You can visualise your home in a crystal pyramid that no one can penetrate (but make sure you allow space for your postman to deliver your post!). You could also plant psychic defence mechanisms around the house, such as strong images of police or potentially aggressive creatures such as lions – or sharks swimming in a moat around your home. Use an image that seems appropriate to you and your property. This doesn't mean to say that when a potential burglar approaches your house, they will physically, or psychically, see the police or animals, but what they will possibly sense is a threat or deeply uncomfortable sensation which will make them want to move on. Do remember to remove those images before you return to your own home, or else you will be made to feel uneasy as you reenter your own place. If in any doubt about whether you've properly removed the protection system, put your own home under a very large white light or a waterfall and cleanse it of previous influences.

Have you gone into your work environment and immediately felt someone around you was in a depressed, withdrawn, or potentially explosive mood? It isn't always appropriate to ask them questions or to try to physically help them in a work place. After all, have you ever turned up for work one day feeling in a vulnerable mood and had a sympathetic colleague throw you an understanding look or give you a gentle hug, prompting you to burst into embarrassed tears? It probably left you feeling worse than ever and certainly more vulnerable. However, you can help without even talking to them. Simply give them a little silent healing, imagining them well and happy, or sending out beams of love and light into their aura. Remember they may not wish to take it but if they do, it's there for them to subconsciously absorb. Again, cleanse as you finish or else you may take on board their symptoms for a while.

Suppose you are cooking a meal for your partner, expecting them home at a certain time. The meal is ready but they don't arrive. You try phoning where you think they ought to be, but there's no reply. Do you turn off the oven or keep the dinner warm or give it to the dog? Before making any decisions, try tuning in to that person and see where they might be. The better you know someone the easier it will be to sense their whereabouts. Try not to let your own thoughts of 'I bet he/she has gone to the so-and-so like they often do' come into it. If you can clear your mind, you may get a sudden, clear flash of where they are.

Conversely, you may be the late party, on your way to see the person with whom you are practising your psychic work. Try sending a message psychically of where you are or how long you will be. Of course, you may have a hard job to penetrate their aura, especially if they're involved in something else at the time, but try and see if you can get through. Remember not to strain too hard to get the information across: relax, breathe deeply and send the message with loving thoughts.

Perhaps you are on your way to an interview in an unfamiliar part of town and as you approach the area, you realise you've forgotten the address which you either had written down somewhere or was in your memory. Don't worry. Take a few deep breaths, close your eyes and concentrate. The information is still within your own aura, you just need to fish it out from the recesses. As soon as you relax, the information will come back to you.

These are all small suggestions of how psychic work can aid you in everyday situations – and there are many more of them. Next time you come across a problem and wonder how to solve it, see if using your psychic development can ease the situation. To ensure your energies don't rebound back at you in an unpleasant fashion, always remember to use them in a loving and gentle way.

Chapter 14: CRYSTAL BALL READING

Crystal ball reading has suffered in the West from being associated with a gypsy in a headscarf, intoning gutturally through a thick accent, usually something along the lines of: 'I see a tall, dark stranger coming into your life. I see travel abroad'. In truth, crystal ball reading, also known as scrying, is an ancient means of psychic expression and many well-known people have used forms of it over the years.

The crystal ball is basically a tool through which you can improve your psychic perception and for centuries, various civilisations have used similar methods. The Babylonians used liquid in sacred bowls into which they gazed, the Hindus preferred a bowl of molasses, the Egyptians used a pool of ink in their hands, and the Greeks lowered mirrors into sacred fountains and springs. Mirror gazing (called catoptromancy) is a form of scrying and was especially popular in the Middle Ages.

John Dee, Scientist and Astrologer to Queen Elizabeth I of England, used crystal balls and a mirror in his work, but no doubt the most famous of all is Nostradamus (1503-66), who predicted in great detail so many of our major world events. Nostradamus favoured a precise form of scrying, using a brass bowl filled with water and then placed on a brass tripod. It was by gazing into this bowl and meditating, that he received unerringly accurate insight into the world's future events.

There is also a detailed account of mirror divination, offered by a Greek traveller, Pausanius, in the second century AD. He was travelling through Patras when he stopped at the Temple of Ceres and stood by a fountain near the temple. He observed that this form of divination was only for the sick, as the afflicted person would first pray to the goddess and offer incense, before letting a mirror down into the fountain by a thread. The mirror was then retrieved and the poor person then looked at his own reflection to ascertain whether death or recovery was imminent!

Another method used was to make a 'black mirror', whereby you take a piece of clock glass, four or five inches in diameter, and paint the outside with black paint.

These early forms of scrying were usually accompanied by an ornate series of rituals, including prayers and fasting. The ball or bowl or mirror was often placed on a 'lamen': an ornate circular table. The table itself then stood within a 'magic circle' on the floor, the circle being an engraved mosaic of mystical names and spiritual images used to enhance psychic work. Some psychics still choose to use a lamen today.

Real crystal balls, made of beryl or quartz, are incredibly expensive and not many can afford to buy them. However, there are various alternative forms of scrying with which you can experiment.

You could try first of all by filling a bowl three-quarters full with water. Choose a bowl that feels right for you, although clear glass will make it easier for you to start. The bowl should be no bigger than four or five inches in diameter and the water should be room temperature. Place the bowl of water on a plain, dark surface, preferably black. If you have a black tablecloth, or piece of black velvet, something that is porous, it will be also help. You may find candlelight a more harmonious means of lighting, or you may find natural light more beneficial (but not strong sunlight). You will have to try different levels of light yourself to see which works for you.

Sit comfortably in front of your bowl. Take some time to concentrate on your breathing and relax. Close your eyes and let the cares of the day wash out of you. Open up in your own time and when you feel ready, open your eyes and gaze into the pool of water. You may see nothing initially, or you may see your own reflection or the reflection of an item near you. You then need to move the position of the bowl until you have as few reflections as possible. Once you have removed the distractions, concentrate again into the pool of water. Try not to stare or push too hard. It needs the same soft gaze as though you were seeing someone's aura for the first time – and the more relaxed you are, the more likely it is you will see something. It may take a while and for that reason it's important you have chosen a comfortable chair in which you can look into the bowl without encouraging backache. You can't rush the process when you first start. Only patience will show you whether scrying could be a useful instrument for you.

If it is going to be a powerful medium for you, you may first of all see a sort of milky fog or cloudy wisps of either black or white. Or you may see the water turn almost black in colour. Or you may be drawn into a reverie where you ponder on something for a while, without quite realising that is what you're doing. Or you may just stare into the water, thinking 'I'm just staring into a bowl of water. This is very boring.' Unless you have the last reaction very strongly, you may find that scrying could be a useful tool for your psychic work. Practise with the water on several occasions before you decide. After a few experiments, you will soon know if it's meant for you.

It's not necessary for you to purchase a real quartz crystal ball at this stage. Glass balls are also highly effective and so are the acrylic (plastic) balls. The latter are easily available on the market and as a beginner, that should be sufficient. Remember, crystal balls are only a tool through which you can improve your psychic abilities. They are not the actual bearers of any information or power. You work through them to increase your own degree of awareness. Of course, you could argue that the better a workman's tools, the more effective his work will be, but all the expensive tools in the world will not help someone who has not properly studied his craft in the first place. That's why, as a beginner, you need not spend a fortune. If you are meant to develop your psychic abilties on this level, then your spirit guides who watch over you will enable you to afford a pure quartz crystal ball in due course, when you are ready for that level of commitment.

Whatever type of ball you purchase, and irrespective of the cost, you should treat it with respect. Always keep it clean and never let anyone else touch it or use it in any way. It should always be kept away from strong light and do also avoid very cold or very hot temperatures. Keep it wrapped in a soft, black cloth when not in use (preferably velvet). If it needs to be cleaned, you're advised to use a weak vinegar and water solution and then polish it dry with a soft velvet cloth or chamois leather.

Some people actually perform a small ceremony to acknowledge their new ball. If this feels right for you, don't be embarrassed to light a candle, say a prayer, or send out some loving vibrations from your aura to the ball itself. You will know from your work with psychometry that all objects become imbued with their own aura, so there is nothing wrong with your wanting to appreciate and acknowledge your new piece of equipment. Also, if your ball has been sitting in a shop for some time, it may have picked up energies from other people passing by. People may even have picked it up and held it for a while. So it's right you should want to cleanse those influences away. Some people believe that placing the ball in moonlight adds to its properties (but, remember, never place it in bright sunlight).

After time working with your own ball, you will develop your own understanding of what you see and what it means. It is really no different that way from psychometry or auric reading, in that you have to learn to interpret what you are picking up on. The difference with a crystal ball reading is that instead of the image flashing in front of your closed eyes or whizzing about in your head, you will actually see the image within the ball. Although every psychic will have their own method of reading a crystal ball, below are a few basic points which may help you as you start.

As you read earlier in this chapter, to begin with you may only see a dense, swirling fog or perhaps small clouds wafting around in your ball. You may stay at this level for a while before you progress. When you do move on, after the clouds, it's likely the ball will then turn black. Only after that will images start to appear. It's sometimes described rather like sequences in a film and they may move slowly or gallop past at some speed.

As a general rule, the left side of your ball, as you look at it, will depict actual scenes or objects in your sitter's life. In other words, it will be their real day-to-day existence. Images on the right are likely to be symbolic and will require some experience and intuition to interpret.

The front of the ball usually represents your sitter's present or immediate future, and the back of the ball either the remote past or distant future. Obviously, part of your progress in working with your ball will be your ability to determine which area of your sitter's life is being shown to you.

Colours are also significant in ball reading and you may see coloured mists during your sitting. As a guide, below is a very basic interpretation of the colours, but, in time, you will develop your own more detailed understanding. You will notice some of the colours may relate to warnings in some aspect of your sitter's life. Remember to always be very careful about how you phrase what you are seeing.

Blue: joy, humour and respect
Green: joy, mediation in some civil matter
Violet: joy, hidden talents to be revealed
Red: danger, trouble or illness. Caution
Orange: Loss, material and spiritual
Yellow: Slander and betrayal. Deceits

These are only a rough guide and you will, through time, have to develop a deeper understanding of what you are seeing. Only practice will deepen your spiritual awareness on this level.

If you want to persevere with crystal ball work but are finding it very difficult to start, here is a method you could try. Sit in front of your ball or bowl of water and make sure you feel comfortable. Now fix your eyes on a bright object in the room for a minute, remembering to breathe deeply and rhythmically. Then close your eyes, turn to face your ball or bowl, and see if you can transfer that image of the object into your ball or water. If that works for you, then try conjuring up a strong image in your mind and transfer that into the ball or water. It's suggested that you choose an image which means something positive and harmonious to you, so that you start by making positive emanations within the ball or water. You shouldn't confuse this with psychically seeing anything; this is purely an exercise to help increase your visualisation technique.

If you do ever have the opportunity to gaze into pure crystal, perhaps in a shop or spiritual fair or even a museum, you will easily be able to appreciate its beauty. As you look into it, you will see a host of different fractures and formations. They're sometimes called 'faerie frost' and they are a glorious myriad of shapes and textures. Just a brief glimpse into quartz crystal and it's almost impossible not to lose yourself in another world. If you ever have the chance to see for yourself, don't miss the opportunity, as it's a wonderful experience.

Chapter 15:
TAROT CARD READING

Tarot Cards are the most widely known form of cartomancy (reading of cards) in psychic work. Basically, a combination of cards is taken from a pack of seventy-eight and these are then laid out in different patterns which the reader uses to contemplate or meditate upon as they give a reading. This can be a very powerful tool for psychics but not everyone is suited to the cards' strong vibrations.

The history of Tarot is very sketchy, with no certainty as to its origin. Some scholars believe the cards derived from the writings of a legendary mystic, Hermes Trismegistus, who was a counsellor of Osiris, King of ancient Egypt. Others believe gypsies carried the cards with them as they wandered across the earth and that they eventually introduced them to Western Europe. It's certainly true that the Hungarian gypsy word for card is 'Tar'. Some say that the ancient city of Fez (now in Morocco) became a centre for philosophers around the world and because everyone spoke different languages, they devised symbolic, pictorial images as a means of communication. It's also interesting to note that during the Renaissance period, there was a custom of using 'ars memorativa' – pictorial memory aids – for meditative purposes. These cards subsequently became part of the occult movement and can be seen on talismans and amulets of the same era. There's no doubt that the Middle Ages were a dangerous time for non-Christians, so it's also possible that Tarot was a way of passing on secret, divine knowledge. By the late sixteenth century, the Tarot cards were being called the 'Devil's Picturebook'.

Despite all the above theories, the earliest physical evidence of any Tarot cards dates from 1392. Seventeen cards are all that remain from the deck and these are kept in a Paris library, although their past history is uncertain. The first full remaining deck dates from the 1420s and it's known that they were painted by an Italian artist, Bonifacio Bembo. They were called the Visconti deck, after the family name of the Duke of Milan who commissioned them.

The uncertain history of the Tarot only adds to its mystery and it's perhaps no coincidence that each card is called an 'Arcanum' – which means mystery. There are twenty-two Major Arcana and fifty-six Minor Arcana. The Minor have four suits of swords, cups, wands and pentacles: a bit like our modern pack of cards. (Sometimes the wands are called batons or the pentacles called coins or rings.) The Major are all symbolic cards, each of which has an individual meaning, a form of divination. They are all 'picture' cards and there's no doubt they have powerful images, some of which you might find disturbing. That is why not everyone finds Tarot a productive tool. However, for others they can be a wonderful means of increasing spiritual awareness. Each card can be interpreted at different levels and, as your mind explores each image, you can go deeper and deeper into uncovering hidden meanings. They say Tarot is the language of the unconscious and, by careful teaching, you can actually open the door into the soul. Therefore, they can be used as a means of uniting man with spirit. Tarot has been likened to a kind of book containing esoteric teachings in visual form. Like all other forms of psychic work, it takes a great deal of study before you reach a high level of proficiency and understanding.

There are also so many different packs of Tarot cards that the choice can be utterly bewildering. There are Chinese, Indian, Greek, Egyptian, Arthurian, Native American packs, even those based on wild animals and herbs. The Rider Waite pack still remains the most commonly used and it is certainly a good start for the beginner.

Before you buy any Tarot cards, however, try to have a look at some first. Perhaps you have a friend or relative who has a set and will let you look through them. Or a New Age shop may have different sets they will let you study. As you look at them, tune in to a card and ask yourself what it means to you. If you find a series of thoughts or images coming into your mind, or the pictures stir your emotions, you may discover they offer you a strong expression of psychic work. The hope is that the pictures will strike hidden, unconscious chords within you. If the sensations you experience are very unpleasant, then you should not consider using them in any form but concentrate on another area of psychic development which suits you better.

If you decide you tune in well with the Tarot cards, then choosing a pack is such a personal matter that there isn't any easy advice. You have to look thoroughly at what is available and then decide what feels right for you. But there is no need to rush the process. They aren't cheap and hopefully whatever you choose will be with you for a long time, so you can afford to look in different shops, at different ranges.

As previously mentioned with the purchase of a crystal ball, you may feel it's right to have a private initiation with your new set of cards. Either light a candle in a private setting, say a prayer, or simply cleanse the pack of cards by placing it in the middle of the pure white energy and have it wash over and through the cards. You may develop some other ceremony that feels right for you.

Each set of cards usually has a brief booklet with it, outlining the meaning of the various cards and what sort of 'spreads' you can use with them. These details tend to be very sketchy and sometimes misleading in their content. You're best advised to purchase a more detailed book separately, or take tuition from an experienced Tarot reader or society. Whatever information you glean for each card, you will, in time, further develop into your own meaning, but you need to have spent some time with each card before you start your readings for other people.

You will find some cards more powerful in their images than others. Those that you feel uncertain about, concentrate on individually. You can do this in different ways. Focus your eyes on the card and try to travel inside it to see what teaching it has to offer you. It's possible that you may gaze at the card and have the scene actually 'come to life' in front of your eyes. Or you can look at the card for a while and then close your eyes, letting your own mind take you on whatever path feels appropriate. Alternatively, leave a card propped up somewhere where you can often see it during the day: by the kettle, on a mantelpiece, or by your desk. Choose a spot that seems comfortable. Then let your gaze fall on the card and leave your subconscious to do the work as you continue on your day's tasks.

When you feel you have developed an empathy with your pack of cards and a sufficient degree of understanding, so that you are ready to offer a sitting to someone, then again be very clear with your sitter about the level at which you can work. Admit honestly that you are a beginner and ask them not to expect too much. Ask them for plenty of feedback at the end, so that you can learn from what they say.

As with all psychic work, create a pleasant environment in which to work and do your best to relax your sitter before you start. You need to relax yourself and then open up and cleanse through as usual. If working with Tarot is going to be powerful for you, you will probably find yourself taking the energy up to the heart chakra without great difficulty. Always remember that as you speak the energy will drop again and you will need to renew again.

When you both feel comfortable, hand your sitter the cards and ask them to shuffle them, however they wish, and for as long as they wish. (This shouldn't be an exercise in endurance – most people shouldn't need to shuffle for longer than a minute or so). If they have a particular aspect of their life about which they want information, ask them to concentrate silently on it while they shuffle. When they are ready, they should stop shuffling and then hand the cards straight back to you. You must not shuffle them after that point or alter their order in any way.

There are so many 'spreads' detailed in so many books that you may not know what to choose as a beginner. Only by studying the different lay-outs will you know what is best for you as a reader. However, there is one spread that you might find helpful as a beginner, given that you have already developed an ability to understand and deal with the chakras. It's called the Chakra Spread and it's a reasonably simple level from which to start.

The Chakra Spread requires seven cards for the seven chakras. Start by turning over the top card in front of you and then add the next directly above it and so on, until you have seven cards facing away from you in a long line. The first card you put down represents the Base, the second the Solar Plexus, the third the Spleen etc, exactly as the chakras in the body. You will, by now, have developed an understanding of each chakra and what it governs in the body and mind but here are a few choice aspects of each card for you to concentrate on:

1 Present material condition surrounding your sitter
2 Their sexuality and their creative potential
3 Their needs, energy and will power
4 Their state of love and harmony
5 Their communication and expression of contact with others
6 Their psychic realm of visualisation and awareness
7 Their ability to draw upon the pure white energy and their spiritual connections

As you are already tuned in to your own chakra system (hopefully!) this may make your early interpretations for others an easier starting point. When you first look at your first card with your first sitter, you may be gripped by a sudden panic of 'not knowing'. After all, looking at the card in front of your sitter is a very different sensation from quietly meditating upon it in your own time. If your mind does go blank or freeze up on you, then look away from the card for a minute, cleanse and keep breathing deeply. Then return your eyes to the card and start again.

If you find yourself working in harmony with the Tarot's vibrations, you will find yourself saying things without really understanding how you know them. It will become a source of strength as well as a powerful learning tool for you and, apart from helping and comforting others, you will have the opportunity to learn a great deal more about your own spiritual path in the process.

Once you are comfortable with the smaller and simpler spreads, there are many more complex and detailed spreads where you can give a reading at a much deeper level.

The Astrological Spread is a good example. This involves the use of twelve cards which have to be spread out as though they were numbers on a large, round clock face. You start at '9pm', the second card is '8pm', and so on until the twelfth is laid down at the '10pm' place. You then give a reading for each card as follows:

1. Your sitter's basic personality
2. Their material possessions, work and values and their attitude towards this part of their life
3. Their communication with their siblings and relatives and early education
4. Their domestic life, referring to home and their mother
5. Their love life, also their creativity and pleasure, also their children and amusements

6 Their work life and day-to-day routines. Also health, diet, exercise and hobbies
7 Their one-to-one relationships, partnership, marriage contracts
8 Their major changes in life, also sex, inheritance and investments
9 Their learning and higher education. Also long-distance travel. Their ideals, dreams, challenges, beliefs and philosophies
10 Achievements and aspirations. Ambitions in career. Also relationship with father
11 Their social life and objectives. Their friends
12 Their mystical life. Their seclusion or escapism. Their faith

You can see that will result in a fairly detailed reading. It also takes experience before you can work comfortably at that level. Remember you can't keep referring to a manual to look at what each card is supposed to tell you about, either in the spread itself, or in your guide to interpreting each card. Don't try to use the cards at this level until you are competent with the smaller spreads.

As with the crystal ball, you shouldn't let your cards be handled by everyone. Apart from your sitter shuffling them, don't let them be touched by other people. You're also advised to cleanse the pack after each sitting. Keep the cards in good condition, clean and unbent, and don't fiddle with them unnecessarily. When they're not in use, store them away safely, preferably wrapped in a soft, dark cloth and away from bright sunlight or extremes of temperature. Don't let them become damp either. Also, don't let children play with them or treat them as a toy. Those powerful images may be distressing for them and give them nightmares. Tarot is an adult tool only.

Chapter 16: THE RUNES

Although not as commonly known as Tarot cards, the Runes are becoming an increasingly popular form of divination. They are a set of twenty-four round, flattened pebbles and onto each is inscribed a different symbol. Some cheaper sets can also be found: they're usually made of plastic and oblong in shape, instead of round. Somewhat like Tarot, each symbol has to be studied and used as a means of expanding consciousness. It's said that the Runes actually define patterns of existence and conciousness that are part of Divine Consciousness and World Being. If that sounds rather heavy, you can settle for describing it as a way to increase spiritual awareness!

Sometimes called the 'Alphabet of Honorius', runic symbols are a combination of Bronze Age carvings and, later, alphabetic scripts. Greek and Latin letters have added their infuence, as well as the German runic alphabet. These symbols and shapes have been found over the years in a wealth of different settings: on huge stone monuments to commemorate events and people, on Viking ships, amulets, weapons, brooches and other items. They've been used for magical and mystical purposes, as well as for warding off evil spirits.

Norse mythology actually states that the Runes are a gift from the God, Odin. The story says that he hung for nine days and nights on the World Tree, whereupon he felt faint and dizzy (which is hardly surprising). He fell from the tree but, as he did so, he saw the Runes and snatched them up. Odin was then re-born with both wisdom and well-being.

Whatever their origin, there is no doubt that the Runes have been used throughout the ages as a source of inspiration and divination. There actually existed Runes Masters and Mistresses who were highly revered within their society.

They kept a pouch containing the stones attached to their clothing, which was very much part of their ritual regalia. These Masters were very powerful people and were regularly consulted about important matters of daily life, such as birth and death, crops, fertility etc.

The twenty-four Runes are separated into three groups, called Freyr, Hagal and Tyr. (In the German runic alphabet, three and eight were considered magical numbers). The Runes are kept within a pouch and then a certain number are chosen carefully by the sitter, one by one, and 'cast' in a variety of ways.

As with Tarot cards, there are a number of sets of Runes available in the shops today and their prices vary enormously. Again, you need to spend some time studying them to know whether they will connect with you on a spiritual level. The plastic sets can be purchased quite cheaply and if you feel this might be a useful tool for you, why not start with the most inexpensive? You will also need a good book on interpretation of the symbols. Most sets come with a small booklet but their meanings barely scratch the surface of the Runes' true significance. It's worth studying the twenty-four shapes in some depth. In this sense, they're less demanding than the Tarot, given there are twenty-four Runes against the seventy-eight cards.

It's also easier to do a reading for yourself with the Runes than with Tarot or crystal ball work. If a friend or relative has a set of Runes, ask if you might try a simple test with them before buying any of your own.

Decide which question you would like to ask: the depth of your question will reflect the depth of your answer. To begin with, try to think of a question that matters to you, without being either trivial ('Should I paint my living room white or pink?') or so profound you will get lost in the response ('Have my partner and I known each other in a former life?'). Think carefully before you settle on a question.

Then, as you concentrate on the question, pick up the bag of Runes with one hand and slowly put your other hand into the bag, letting the Rune stones run through your fingers. If they are made of smooth stone, that alone can be a very pleasant experience. Don't look at any of them but feel with your fingers which one you want to pull out. You will probably find you are drawn to one stone without having to concentrate. Without looking at the stone, place it down in front of you. Open your eyes. If the stone is blank, you have either drawn out the blank Rune or the symbol is on the other side. Turn the stone over without too much thinking and then leave it. Don't turn the stone round to make it what you think is 'right-side up' because some symbols have a 'reversed' meaning and you may be meant to read this instead. Then use the book to see which symbol you've chosen and read what it says about it – remembering to use the reversed definition if that is the way you turned it over.

As there are so many different books offering varying interpretations (some of them very 'deep' and requiring a lot of study), you will find it isn't easy to get a quick answer to your question. However, if you spend some time meditating upon what you read in relation to your question, you may find the words enlightening.

You can also do a more detailed analysis by choosing three Runes in the same way (without looking) and then laying the three stones out in a row from left to right. To interpret your question, the first Rune on the left is the situation as it stands at present, the second (middle one) is what action you need to take, and the third (on the right) is the final outcome. Reading about these three Runes in succession may give you a greater understanding of what is going on in your life.

If you choose to buy the Runes and offer them for use in a sitting, then you may wish to go through the same process as with a crystal ball or Tarot cards. Have a small ceremony in your own way, cleansing the Runes and blessing them, before you offer them in a sitting. After a sitting, once they've been handled by someone else, you may also think about cleansing them again. Keep them away from people when not in use, again wrapping them in soft, dark material and keeping them in a cool, dry place.

The Runes differ from the Tarot in the sense that the images are not as immediately powerful and thought-provoking. Therefore, it is the books which analyse the symbols that are your guide and you may have to read through a few before you find one that you find inspirational and mind-expanding. Provided you find a book which suits you, the Runes can be a good tool for psychics.

As with Tarot, when giving a sitting, you need to cleanse and open up. Taking your energy up to the solar plexus or spleen is the highest you need in this work but, as always, you need to be as relaxed as possible. Once your sitter has chosen their Runes and cast them (using any of a variety of patterns detailed in books), you need to be open and tuned in to read the particular Runes' interpretations. Initially, you may have to refer to the book and read aloud to your sitter what has been written but, then, if the Runes are a positive instrument for you, you should be able to expand on what you have read and offer further details on the question they wish answered. Again, as with Tarot and the crystal ball, the Runes don't have power in themselves. It's up to you to interpret powerfully what is there if you are going to provide inspiration for your sitter. Anyone can read from a book, after all.

The Runes can, therefore, seem a slower form of psychic development but if you have the ability to purchase an inexpensive set, it is worth having them around you as a tool that you can practise with on occasion.

As with any learning process, expanding your psychic awareness can seem to become stagnant if you concentrate on only one area, such as just psychometry and nothing else. Don't be hesitant to try out different methods and don't feel discouraged if some have no real power for you. Experimentation is good for beginners. In fact, it's essential, as a means of you discovering what is right for you.

Chapter 17:
SUMMING UP AND LOOKING AHEAD

If this is the first time you have read through this book, and you have managed to retain a third of what you have read, then you are doing extraordinarily well! To properly develop your psychic skills you need a good basic understanding of what you are trying to do, and then a lot of patience and determination to practise and increase your awareness.

You may think you have remembered all the salient points through the chapters and that you are more than prepared to work effectively. However, do have a read through the following points. Think through each section thoroughly and don't rush it. Do you really understand it all? Are you sure? If there are areas you still haven't grasped, then you could benefit from some re-reading.

Psychic work has immeasurable benefits but it's not a 'plaything'. Ask yourself if you truly understand why you must treat your sitters and all psychic phenomena with the greatest respect and sensitivity.

Psychic development is enhanced by full comprehension of how it works. Check you know the seven chakras with their relevant locations and colours, then go through the various energies used in psychic work, and finally define the word 'aura'.

The cleansing process is as vital as the opening and closing processes. Go through all three and see if you can remember everything clearly without having to refer back to earlier chapters.

An auric reading is a good start for the beginner. See if you can remember how to tune in on an auric level and think about the sort of information you can pick up. Also reflect on what you can't do with an auric reading.

Psychometry can offer very strong vibrations. Describe how this process works and why it isn't a good idea to use certain items.

Flower reading works on a deeper, more spiritual level than auric work and psychometry. Be clear about why this is the case, and then go through the various parts of the flower, remembering to what aspect of life each relates.

Healing is a particularly powerful area of psychic work. Describe how the process works and why absent healing can also be beneficial. Remember to include the importance of constant cleansing and mention the two areas of the body on which you shouldn't linger.

Psychic drawing can be a helpful tool for releasing energy and increasing psychic awareness. Recap on how it works, including the meanings of the seven chakra colours and how you might define different shapes in drawings.

Learning psychic defence techniques is essential if you intend to pursue psychic development. List at least ten ways in which you can protect yourself.

Crystal balls, Tarot cards and Runes can all be useful tools in psychic work. See if you can describe the basic concept of each and how they work.

Have you discovered you remember less than you thought from the entire book?

If you answered 'yes' to that question, then you are probably going to do well in developing your psychic abilities. If you answered 'no' you are either possessed of a photographic memory or not being truthful!

The fact is that you won't find this book or any book an instant recipe for success because psychic work cannot operate on that level. What you can do is develop a basic understanding and gradually increase your awareness – and your gifts – from that starting point. If reading this book has made you want to learn more and develop your skills, then you can do so in a variety of ways.

Firstly, read anything and everything about subjects relating to psychic and holistic matters. Attend as many lectures, workshops, weekend seminars, spiritual fairs, festivals and retreats as you possibly can. No one should ever tell you that psychic work can only operate in one way and under a certain set of guidelines. It is such a complex subject that you can approach it from many different angles and decide for yourself what best suits you.

Don't limit yourself to just psychic phenomena either. As the psychic operates very much on a spiritual and holistic realm, look into other related subjects. There are so many! To name but a tiny handful in random order: colour therapy, crystals, aromatherapy, homeopathy, holistic massage, acupuncture, Alexander technique, meditation, Kirlian photography, yoga, Feng Shui, astrology, Theosophy, graphology, numerology, Tai Chi, astral travel, Qigong, dowsing and Reiki. You may already have a cursory knowledge of some of the above but others you may not even have heard of before. Spend any free time you might have in health and new age shops, browsing through book shelves and looking at new products on offer. Start discussing the concepts of spirituality/karma/re-incarnation with friends and relatives. You'll probably be amazed that people you thought completely unconnected with psychic work have, in fact, had an interest for quite a while. For every disinterested sceptic, there will be an open-minded listener. A fascinating aspect of psychic work is that once you open your mind to other possibilities, you seem to attract other like-minded people to you.

There's little doubt that the best way to improve your psychic abilities, so that you progress to a deeper level with safety and protection, is to join a development circle. This is a group of other novice psychics who sit in a mutually supportive group, run by an experienced psychic of some years' experience. You can progress at a greater rate when under guided tuition because you will feel safe, supported and nurtured. This is assuming that the teacher has brought the right group of people together, whose energies are compatible and who are all sincere in their aim to learn. Provided they have created this atmosphere from the beginning, there is no reason why you couldn't stay within such a group for years as you gradually learn the art of psychic development.

How can you find such a circle? There are a growing number of psychic and spiritualist organisations around the world and if you contact any one of them, they will no doubt let you know whether they are able to offer a place to a newcomer. They may not be in a rush to take you on and nor should you rush into any circle without consideration first. Always meet the teacher before committing yourself and use your own tuning-in process to see if you feel comfortable with them and the organisation to which they belong. Finding the right development circle is no different from choosing the right home or partner or job: it may take some time and soulsearching! But if you can find the right group for you, there is no other single, more powerful choice you could make to improve your psychic development.

If you found this book interesting but are uncertain or sceptical about its content, then it will still have benefited you in some way. You probably won't have any desire to develop your psychic potential, but that simply means it isn't the right time for you to do so. What may happen, as a result of your digesting some new concepts, is that you find yourself being more aware of other people and atmospheres around you. You may not be consciously aware of it yourself, but those close to you will sense a difference, and this increased awareness can only benefit you and others.

As human beings, we are much more complicated – and wonderful! – than we generally acknowledge. This book is intended for all of you who feel that way instinctively, but rarely take the time to think about it in more detail. Enjoy

your psychic and spiritual growth, and may the protective spirits above you, guide and bless you on each step of your journey.